STITCHED
MIXED
MEDIA

JESSICA GRADY

STITCHED MIXED MEDIA

THE CROWOOD PRESS

CONTENTS

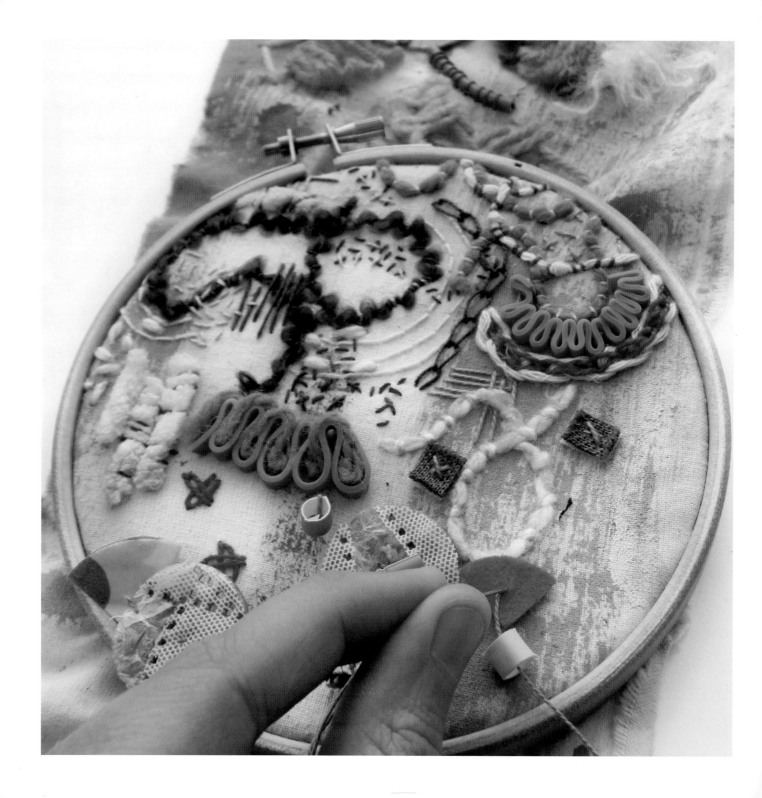

INTRODUCTION

This book is designed to help you find creative ways to utilise a range of different materials to start exploring mixed media and stitch. Whether you are a complete beginner or someone who wants to expand upon their techniques and skills further, there will be something exciting within these pages to get the creative inspiration flowing.

As an artist, materials fascinate me, and they are often the source of my inspiration for new projects. I enjoy using media that is not often considered with textile practices, particularly recycled materials. Rather than looking at something as it is now, what I like to do is think about its future potential after it has been creatively transformed. If that material is a piece of rubbish that can be repurposed into a new life, even better. Transforming mixed media is where the magic happens; even something as simple as chopping a circle out of a rectangular piece of packaging and – *ta-dah!* – you have your very own handmade sequin! You can transform mixed media materials in many ways including manipulation, folding, pleating, scrunching, painting, layering, cutting and rolling, to name a handful. If you run all these lovely transformations through your head when you next see something interesting, it will help you to think about a material's future potential as an embellishment. My aim as an artist is for my finished samples or ideas (using any material) to have a playful hint towards their origins, but you have to really look closely to discover what they used to be.

Examples of a colourful selection of mixed media materials to transform into handcrafted embellishments, including painted papers, fabric scraps, recycled metal sheets, waste plastics and foam shapes.

The layout of this book is structured by materials, therefore you can really get into the fine detail of each medium as a single idea before developing and combining materials and techniques to create your own unique samples. I use the techniques explored in this book to create my own artwork and textile sample library. I am very much of the belief that stitch and mixed media is such a fun, exciting and accessible craft to get involved with. My work is driven by process and the idea of really enjoying the making, the exploring and the

A stitched sample in progress, looking at colour, texture and materials.

In my studio, looking through textile samples.
(Photo: Christian Ståhle)

A mixed pile of handcrafted embellishments, ready for stitching onto base materials. Having a prepared stash of embellishments to hand will give you inspiration for new ideas and samples.

experimenting, as this is most often when the unexpected serendipity happens. I truly believe that you cannot create something wrong, as everything can be used in some capacity; and anything that you create that you aren't as keen on can be chopped up, painted over and repurposed into something new.

There is also lots of room within this book for you to take my ideas, techniques and suggestions, and allow them to flourish and bloom into your own developments, without the end results being limited by a purely textile outcome. Whether you like painting, making your own clothing or journalling, or are a craft dabbler and like a bit of everything, mixed media and stitch can be added in, to transform your ideas into something new.

The simple act of sitting with a needle and thread and stitching is such a relaxing and enjoyable way to destress and unwind. I particularly enjoy the sound of a sharp needle punching through a drum-tight piece of fabric with that lovely pop. Remember, the journey of making and creating is the most special and rewarding part. So, begin the journey, let it lead you to unexpected places and enjoy!

A selection of mixed media samples demonstrating the range of ideas and techniques explored within this book. This wide variety shows the scope and possibilities of embracing and trying out new materials combined with hand stitching.

CHAPTER 1

BEGINNINGS

Getting started with a new creative practice, technique or idea is often the most difficult part. This first chapter will look at ways to prepare, and get you started to explore some new ideas and techniques with creative textiles and mixed media embellishments.

BASIC SUPPLIES TO COLLECT

Sometimes the simplest of materials and supplies can be the most versatile. Having some of these staple items in your craft cupboard or studio will help you with many of the techniques and ideas demonstrated within this book. Personally I find it very helpful to collect and source my basics first before starting anything new. I think that it is not always about buying the most expensive or name-branded products – you can source a lot of materials around your own home to repurpose. You also do not always need everything on the list; feel free to swap and change materials based on your access and personal preferences.

Sewing Needles

An absolute staple for any textile enthusiast, I have hundreds and hundreds of sewing needles and would highly recommend having a few packs of varying sizes. My favourites are sharps and tapestry needles. Most people will automatically go for a

My tool kit of basic materials that I use for stitching and sampling. Perle cotton threads come in handy balls, rather than looped skeins, and don't tangle as easily. A needle book is also useful as it stops loose needles from rattling around.

sewing needle with a very large eye, even when using a narrow thread. My advice is to always go for the smallest needle you can get away with. The smaller the needle, the easier it will be to pull through your base, and you will also have more versatility for adding on small embellishments such as beads. Particularly when using mixed media and more unconventional items, a small-eyed, thin needle such as a sharp will

Clipping sheets of materials into bundles creates mini sketchbooks of details and ideas to help you get started.

equal less sore fingers! A child's plastic embroidery needle is great to have to hand for experimenting with large, chunky threads and going through bases with large holes.

Scissors or Cutters

Having separate pairs of scissors for cutting different materials will be very handy and saves you from ruining any expensive fabric scissors. Cutting through recycled and thicker materials, including metals, plastics and thick fabrics, can quickly blunt scissor blades. Glue and tape will also gum up them up. Another handy basic is to have a pair of thread cutters or snips. These can be used specifically for trimming the ends of your threads when stitching and are often small and compact, so are good to pack for portable projects.

Glue and Tape

I don't love using glue, but there is no denying it can be a very helpful addition for fixing the placement of embellishments, finishing edges or even adding special finishes or preserving raw materials before they are transformed into embellishment ideas. I normally have a glue stick, white glue or PVA, fabric glue, paper tape and double-sided tape in my supplies box. Masking tape in particular is excellent for marking out sample sizes, and often the cheaper brands are lower tack, meaning they are easier to peel off fabric without furring or adding pulls on the surface.

Sewing Threads

The choice of sewing threads can be very overwhelming. Branded thread is not always necessary, particularly when you are first trying a new craft or practising with sample pieces. I tend to look at the composition of a thread rather than its brand name. I like using 100 per cent cottons, which can come in bright, matte vibrant tones, or lustrous mercerised cotton, which has a shine to it.

For a beginner I would recommend looking at Perle cottons in no. 8 weight, rather than stranded cotton. Perle cotton can be used exactly as it is, whereas stranded cotton, which is sold in skeins, has to be split into sections as it can be too thick to stitch with as a single thread, especially when using embellishments.

Silk and metallic sewing threads may look very tempting as they come in luscious colours, silky and shiny, but they can also be a complete nightmare to work with. They are great to experiment with for quality of finish as you grow in confidence. Having a great basic sewing thread in your kit is going to give you more versatility for exploring and developing samples.

Base Materials

As with embroidery thread, having a staple base material in your supply list will make life easier for you when it comes to exploring new ideas and techniques. Remember that this does not have to be textile based, but fabric is a good starting point as it is the most familiar of materials for most stitchers. The base you stitch onto can really help or hinder you. I look out for several things when sourcing new bases to work with: base thickness, flexibility and opacity are all key factors. A good beginner's base material wants to be mid-weight with a texture that isn't too thick or too thin, such as cotton, denim or thin cardboard. Always test to ensure that you can easily pull your sewing needle through without much effort.

If you use a fabric or a material that is very flexible, I would advise using an embroidery hoop to keep the material tight and flat when stitching. Thick paper or thin card is also a good base as it is very easy to source, and the stiffness will mean you can stitch it without needing an embroidery hoop. Opaque bases that are a solid colour, such as most natural textiles and papers or cards, are also good basics. Transparent materials are very fun but can be tricky, especially when you need to consider the threads moving through the base as you can see both sides at once. For fabrics, natural textiles such as cotton, linen and canvas are all easier to stitch through and work with than synthetics.

Embroidery Hoops

Embroidery hoops are a great basic for any stitcher to have. They really help with reducing any puckering or ripples on the base material when stitching and make it easier to add

Selection of embroidery hoops, including bamboo, plastic, painted and wrapped hoops. I would recommend wrapping any hoop with a strip of thin fabric before use, as this will help to ensure the base material you put inside the hoop will not slip.

a plastic tile spacer. Embellishments can be two- or three-dimensional and any size, shape or material.

Having a basic collection of materials to create embellishments with is not as complicated as it may appear. There is lots of potential for various mixed media that will be expanded upon in the following chapters. You can start with a handful of these materials, perhaps thinking about different sources in order to really experiment with your results. If you get stuck with choice I would recommend using what you already own and choosing colours and textures that you enjoy.

- Papers or cardboard
- Fabrics
- Metal
- Recycled plastic
- Found materials from nature

GETTING INSPIRATION

Often the act of collecting your supplies to start a project or idea can generate that inspiration or excitement to get going and start making. However, sometimes it doesn't. When I need a little extra push to help me out with those first few stages, I simplify the process into colour and shape. This could be choosing one specific colour or colour palette and only creating a sample using those colours. Or sometimes it could be the opposite: deliberately *not* choosing a colour palette and putting together whatever comes to hand.

When thinking about shape, I go for the basics such as circles, squares or triangles. The beauty of simple shapes is the amazing potential to create so many different outcomes. I would avoid the idea of creating a 'picture' – this can put lots of pressure on yourself to make the perfect image that you have envisaged in your head, and it can prevent you from really experimenting and playing with embellishments and stitch. The best tip I can offer is to just go for it! The aim is not perfection, it is to express creativity and start the development process.

embellishments. Hoops tend to be sized in inches, and a great hoop size for creating samples is 5–6in (13–15cm) in diameter – this is large enough to create a good-sized sample.

Hoops can come in a variety of materials and forms, including wooden, plastic and even metal. I would recommend a basic bamboo embroidery hoop, which will have an adjuster on the top to tighten the tension of your base. The bamboo hoops are very lightweight and will accommodate a wide variety of materials. I always use an embroidery hoop when stitching with fabric and plastic bases. For stiffer materials, such as paper or metal, you will not need a hoop.

Mixed Media Embellishment Materials

An embellishment is anything that you feel will add a decorative element to a base and can be attached in place, generally with stitch. A traditional embellishment is something like a sequin that you might find at a haberdashery store. Finding and making your own embellishments is much more rewarding. This could be something that can be cut out and stitched in place, such as a sheet of coloured paper, or an object such as

SOURCES FOR MIXED MEDIA MATERIALS

A question that I am asked time and time again is: 'Where do you collect and source your unusual materials?' The answer is, very simply, everywhere! Beginning with the ordinary items you have at home is good practice for collecting resources. Look at the food packaging that you see in the supermarket, your favourite jumper that has a hole in it, or the elastic bands the postman wraps around your post. Even when going out for a walk in your local environment, can you spot a rusty washer on the pavement or an interestingly shaped leaf or seed pod? As you start to recognise what you like to use and what works well, this will lead you to think about other sources.

I am a huge fan of scrapstores and secondhand shops. Scrapstores are located across the UK and many are run by local councils or are CICs (community interest companies). They aim to take safe, reusable waste – often from industry – and resell it to groups, individuals, charities, schools or whoever can make use of it. For craft purposes it's fantastic, as stock is quite heavy with textiles, thread and paper. Stock changes constantly as supplies are used up and new waste comes in, meaning you always have fresh, exciting materials to work with.

I often find a lot of dead-stock in scrapstores. This is the term for materials that a company has been unable to sell for a variety of factors. Most of the time there are no flaws whatsoever with dead-stock and often this dead-stock is sent

Some examples of collected items from scrapstores. I have transformed many of these items further with paint, dye and pattern. You can see the negative offcuts from industrial production, which make great bases for weaving and twisting threads in and out.

to landfill if it cannot be sold. To give you an idea of the variety of treasure you can find, these are some items I have found previously in my local scrapstore: leftover neon vinyl from fire engine signage, waste circles of neoprene from a wetsuit factory, rolls of dead-stock lace and a giant bag of felt washers from industrial machinery. The best thing of all about using scrapstores is that you are saving material from being thrown away and preventing that waste from going to landfill, so it's a win-win situation. If you don't have a scrapstore near you, any other secondhand shops or resources are always great to look out for. Remember that you can wash, chop up, colour and transform old items to make them new again – it's all about that potential.

STORAGE AND ORGANISATION

Once you start collecting different materials, the issue can be how to store them in an accessible way that doesn't take up too much space, where it is easy to see what you want to use. There are three main ways I organise supplies: by the types of mixed media materials, their sizes or their colours.

Washed-out spice jars filled with small embellishments. From left to right: striped plastic sequins, painted plastic sequins, paper and foil scraps, tiny metal washers and collected plastic lids.

A display of bulldog-clipped samples of materials. You can see where I bundle similar colours together and where I make appealing texture combinations by putting contrasting materials together as inspiration for creating new sample ideas.

FIVE TOP TIPS FOR ORGANISING MATERIALS

1. Save your old spice jars for small items – as these are clear, you can easily see what is inside. Wash them out and fill them with shells, thread ends, small scraps of fabric or cut-out shapes. Pop them in a spice rack for storage.

2. Use large bulldog clips to bundle together collections of materials that you find really interesting or would like to work with in your next project. I often do this for materials that I have transformed and for my sequin sheet offcuts. I also put these up on my studio wall for inspiration – I can quickly snip a corner off a piece of dyed fabric to use in a sample.

3. For larger sheets or pieces of material, such as a bundle of papers or packets of food wrappers, cardboard folders containing different materials can be useful. As well as organising these by material, another solution is to organise by colour, so keep all similar colours together in the same folder or box. This can be helpful when starting a project.

4. When collecting recycled plastic wrappers from food or packaging, I fold these up and place them inside a clear cereal box liner. I keep this in a drawer in my kitchen and add to it when I have more wrappers to put inside.

5. Plastic vegetable trays from mushrooms or tomatoes are fantastic for smaller items. I have several and like to keep one on my desk for storing small offcuts. They make great paint palettes and the plastic itself can be cut up or painted to make more sequins.

I keep a jar to hand to fill with snips of thread; either the frayed edges from fabrics, the cut ends from knotting the back of samples or any that are too tangled to use. The result is this jar of colour that can be used for many different samples.

A jar of colourful striped recycled plastic sequins.

CHAPTER 2

STITCH AND THREAD

Hand stitching is a mindful and methodical process that is steeped in tradition. I enjoy the process of hand stitching as it gives me complete control over how an embellishment is going to be attached to my base, as well as adding a decorative element and pattern to a sample. Stitching an embellishment into position also means it is secure and easy to reattach if it does come loose, without risk of damage. It's not about knowing how to create hundreds of complex hand embroidery stitches, it is having a solid foundation of basic stitches. This will give you the most versatility for making the stitches your own, being able to experiment with unconventional thread ideas and making those stitches a reflection of your creativity, while inspiring you to develop new ideas.

There is a common misconception that embroidery stitches have to look pristine and pin neat on the back of your base material. This can turn people away from trying out hand stitching, as they worry it won't be correct or properly done. I don't think a stitch can be created incorrectly; it is your own journey and interpretation, and I love a messy stitched back! For me, the travelling of threads across the back of a piece of fabric or paper really shows the work and energy that has gone into creating that sample or artwork.

BUILDING A FOUNDATION OF SIMPLE STITCHES

The best way to start anywhere is with the basics. Having your foundation of simple stitches in place will give you more versatility and opportunity for developing those stitches. There are so many ways that you can change a simple stitch to make it look more contemporary and exciting. I like to visualise my stitching as making marks; depending on if I am looking for straight lines, curved lines, dots or loops will change the stitch I use to create that mark. It can be helpful to practise by drawing stitches as lines and shapes on paper – this is a brilliant way to really visualise how embroidery is linked to pattern, texture and doodling. My library of flexible stitches includes four staple basics, which all can be created in multiple ways: straight stitch, couching, chain stitch and French knots.

A hand embroidery stitch can be pulled through a base material using a single thread type. For some stitches, such as couching, one thread type can sit on the surface of the base material with a secondary thread going through the base and securing the top thread in position. These two methods mean that any thread that is too thick to pull through the base can still be used as a thread and instead can sit securely on top.

All of the basic stitches that I have in my stitch library can be utilised for securing embellishments. When creating a sample with embellishment details, I always try to make my stitches work in multiple ways. This means that you may think about adding your stitches so that they are very visible and

A selection of stitched doodle samples. Each one uses simple stitches in a variety of ways to create a highly textured and patterned surface.

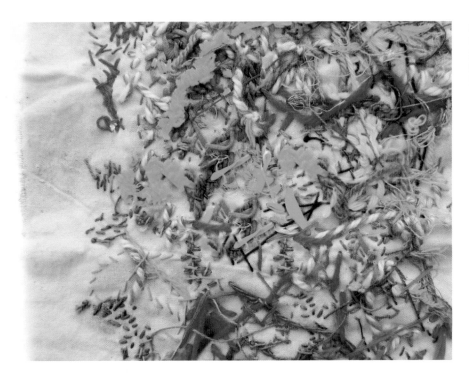

An example of the underside of a stitched sample. You can see the chaotic crossover of threads and the different colours and patterns that look completely different to the front side of the sample.

Textile sample showcasing embellishments secured with bright contrasting threads that pull out additional details and patterns.

provide extra detail and pattern on your sample. If you are stitching on your embellishments, why not make the most of the effort that has gone into the stitches and make it a feature of your sample too?

The variables to change a stitch's appearance and pattern can be broken down into the main areas of: base material, thread type, stitch length, stitch scale, stitch spacing and stitch direction. Changing your base material will affect what threads can be used. If you use something clear as a base, you will be able to see the back of your stitches as well as the front. Other bases that are not fabric, such as paper, recycled plastic or even metal, can be prepunched with a needle and your stitches have to be more planned out. The base material will most affect the stability of your stitches, as you need something that is going to hold your thread, stitches and any embellishments that you choose to add.

Regarding thread types, anything that can be made into a thin strip or length can be used as a thread. Your thread choice is one of the main ways to alter the texture and colour of your embroidery stitches.

The other variables – stitch length, scale, direction and the spacing in-between each stitch – all help to shape the pattern that you create with your stitches. Stitches can be layered up together, pulled apart in micro scale, created in rhythmic lines or echo the shapes of embellishments or patterned bases. Playing with simple stitch ideas before adding embellishments can be a great way to get your inspiration flowing. It can also build up samples that you can work back into or use as a guide for your stitches in future practice.

Unconventional thread ideas. From top left you can see: crepe paper, garden twine, mesh ribbon, felt selvedge, plastic strips, dyed string, shower puff, cotton tape, parcel twist, electric cables, elastic bands, florist ribbon, cotton T-shirt, earth cable sleeve, pipe cleaner and dyed medical tubing. All these threads create different tactile qualities that add new textures to the stitches they are created with.

UNCONVENTIONAL THREAD IDEAS

Thread type is really interesting to experiment with. Embroidery cotton such as Perle is great to have in your tool box and is very useful as a basic thread, but is not the only material that can be used to stitch with. In fact, your thread does not have to be a 'thread' in the traditional sense at all! Try envisaging thread as a fairly thin, flexible strip of anything. Having this mindset can open up endless possibilities. Any large sheet of material such as paper, fabric, recycled plastic or even metal can be turned into a thread by simply cutting the material into

a long thin strip. You can then use this as a flat strip, or twist or roll to create a more textured chunky thread idea. Having a large-eyed, sharp tapestry needle or a children's plastic needle will be helpful for chunky, unusual threads.

Most unconventional threads that are not easy to pull through your base material due to their width, stiffness or texture can all still be successfully used by pairing them with a couching stitch. Using couching in this way means you can stitch with materials that would never be able to be pulled though the eye of a needle. A good idea for trialling any unconventional threads is to always try with a fabric base of natural material with a large weave structure. This will be easier to use than something synthetic that may rip or tear.

I often visit my local garden centre or DIY shop if I am looking for some new unusual thread inspiration. Plant wire, cable sleeve, plumbing tubing or cable ties are all great items to try out, which are a little more unusual. I also like using elastic bands, hair bobbles, bag ties, fishing line, washing line rope, strimmer line and paper straws. Wire in particular is a great

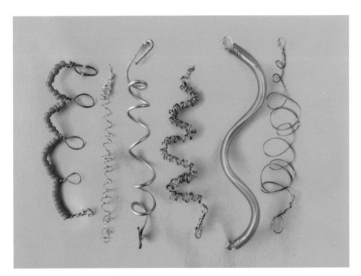

Stitched wire samples on leatherette. You can see how the wire has been twisted and looped into different shapes. The thinner wire will create a tight corkscrew curl and can also be used to add beads, or even threaded through another material, such as plastic tubing, to give it structure. The thicker wire has a more 3D graphic look on the sample.

thread as it bends and creates structure and shape, and you can find a huge array of widths and colours. Some wire is fine enough to pull through the fabric as a traditional thread. Other varieties can be couched into position and stitched over to make shapes. I enjoy circling and bending my wire into shapes, adding loops so that it adds a 3D element to my stitches. You can also embellish your wire before using it by threading on small beads or wrapping with another thread to ramp up your pattern even more.

The most important factor when looking at unconventional threads is to be playful and think outside the box. Even if something doesn't work, it can lead your work in new directions.

STRAIGHT STITCH

Straight stitch is the most basic of hand embroidery stitches. It involves creating a line on the surface of your base by pushing a needle and thread in and out of the material. You can also use a straight stitch to attach embellishments by pushing your needle through your base, then an embellishment, then back through your base again. The simplicity of a straight stitch is what makes it so easy to manipulate. As long as you always follow the 'in and out' pattern, making sure the needle goes from the front of the base to the back, then the back of the base to the front, a straight stitch cannot go wrong. Creating a sample just using variations of straight stitch can help to get ideas flowing. It can also create a lovely base that you can work back into with other stitches or embellishments in the future. A straight stitch underpins many other stitches that are all made up of this simple technique.

- Straight stitch does not always have to follow a straight line. You could change the appearance of your stitch by creating zigzags, crosshatched areas or layered textured patterns, which still all use the basis of a straight line stitch – I think of it as stitch doodling. This can change the density of your stitches.

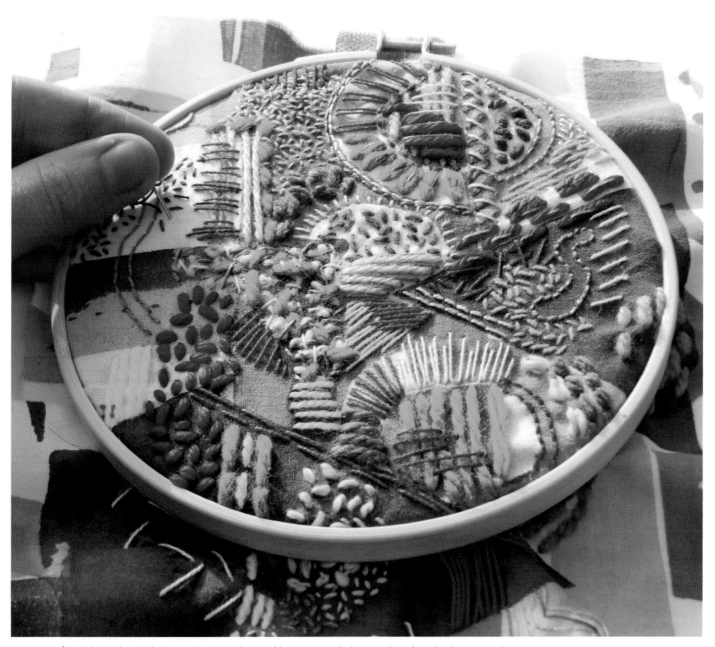

Variations of straight stitch sample in progress using the variables mentioned, changing length, scale, direction and spacing. This is a great foundation idea to try.

- Shrinking down your straight stitch into tiny lines to create seed stitches is a great one for adding texture and pattern to a larger area. It is also a great idea for scattering across flat embellishments such as cut shapes of paper, recycled plastic or fabric.
- Big chunky threads such as ribbon, wool and trims add texture to a sample when used with straight stitch. If you find a thicker thread more difficult to pull through a base, when you pull through the thread, give the needle a wiggle as you pull thorough the eye to widen the hole in the base.
- Stitching straight stitches close together with small gaps can create curved and complex shapes. You can draw with your needle and thread around a pattern or shape on your base.

- Once you have a simple line of straight stitches in place on your base, you can play around with looping and weaving threads under and over the lines of stitch, using your straight stitch as your anchor.
- Supersize straight stitches by looping thick cord, strips of fabric or washing line through a base with large holes, such as a plastic mat or mesh fabric. You don't even need to use a needle but can use your fingers to pull threads through to create the stitches.
- Embellish your straight stitches with beads or small sequins. Thread your embellishments onto your stitch as it sits on the base surface, and then go through the base to the other side as usual, to complete the stitch.

Further straight stitched line samples, including using the stitch as an anchor thread to loop and wrap other threads into position. This gives a more textured appearance as the looped thread is bouncing away from the surface, or pulling the thread tight to create a more structured pattern.

COUCHING

Couching is a stitch technique that will really expand your imagination to the possibilities of threads. It involves two threads: a thin thread such as a Perle, which is pulled through the base as a straight stitch, and a thicker thread of any width, thickness or material that sits on the base surface and is 'couched' into position. The thin thread is stitched over the thicker thread to create small vertical stitches on a horizontal thread. This is traditionally created so that the thread lays flat, but tweaking this to create more 3D and tactile variations can be exciting. There are a few different ways to think about couching: one that creates textured 3D qualities and another that creates more patterned lines and shapes. Both are very useful to pair with embellishments and can enhance and add details to samples.

Simple Couching

Simple couching can be used to create very intricate patterns with endless loops, scrolls and swirls as well as lettering and angular geometrics, or for use with stiff materials that don't flex or bend. I like to use couching to get an energetic sense of drawing on fabric with stitch. Begin by laying down your thicker thread on the base. Then carefully stitch over this thread to contain it, with smaller straight stitches in a thinner thread to secure the shape to the base.

- Practise simple couching with easy threads such as wool, which will stay in the shape that you manipulate when you lay it on the base material, and can be easily secured in place with your couching stitch over the top.
- Experiment with the gaps of the couching, creating layered patterns by changing the width of the couching all the way around the thicker thread.

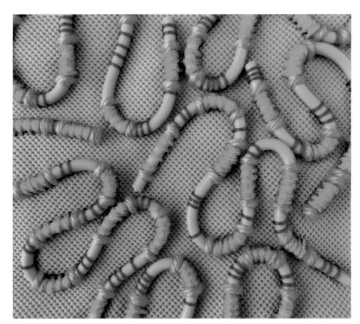

Couching example using recycled electric cables with wool and cotton threads. The wires snake across the fabric base to create pattern and shape.

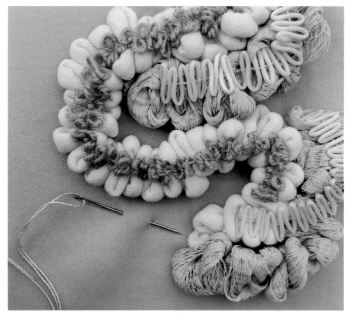

Ruffled couching example with a highly textured feel. The thread is raised off the surface for a bold, chunky look.

- Playing with multiple threads and colours can create more interest by adding in stripes to your thicker thread that is being couched. Contrasting threads will add zing and sharpness to your couching, whereas tonal threads will create a more invisibly attached shape.
- As well as creating your couching by going across the thicker thread in a straight line, change the angle of the thread to create a zigzag or go back over with another thread for a crossed design.
- If you are couching a more complex shape or pattern with lots of movement, add in securing stitches along the key points of the thicker thread first with your thin thread. Then go back along the shape and infill with the rest of the stitches to complete.

- To create more 3D simple couched effects, stitch an area secure and then pull or twist the thicker thread away from the base and continue to stitch flat. Small areas when completed will stand vertically off the base, but are still stitched securely in position. This is great to try with stiffer threads with structure such as wire, recycled plastic tape, gift ribbon or paper strips.

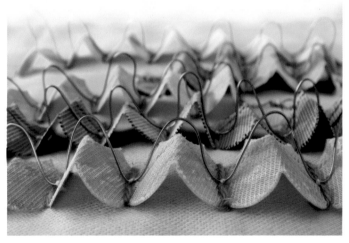

Detail of couched sample, using folded plastic strips and wire to create a 3D texture on the fabric surface.

Couching example – small beads and plastic thread have been used to secure the recycled plastic canisters, whilst adding patterns to the sample.

How to Create Ruffle Couching using Two Different Threads

This is a great technique for introducing texture to a base surface. Once you have tried the stitch, it is very easy to adapt and experiment with other wools, ribbons, paper twists and thin pieces of fabric. You can explore and sample ideas, depending on your project. The finished stitch sits on the base with a ruffled, loopy finish; it is ideal for both going around curved shapes and for straight lines or lettering. It is a quick and simple method to build up the surface with a 3D quality, and a fantastic way to experiment with any tricky yarns, wools or threads that are difficult to pull through the base as a normal stitch.

MATERIALS NEEDED

- Base material: a fabric in any colour or type is great to start with.
- Small-eyed sharp needle and scissors.
- Embroidery thread in any colour, three strands of thread or a Perle cotton.
- Two threads for ruffle couching, such as: elastic bands, wool, ribbon, braiding, cut strip of fabric, cords, garden twine. These threads have to be thick and easy enough for a needle to stitch through the centre of the thread.
- Embroidery hoop, large enough to fit your base securely.

1. Secure your base material in an embroidery hoop. Pull a small-eyed needle, threaded with embroidery cotton, through your base. Ensure your thread is anchored with a large knot.

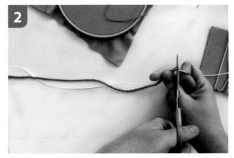

2. Cut two lengths of thick thread. These can be whatever size you wish, but a good starting guide is approx. 30cm (12in).

3. Thread the end of the two threads onto the needle, going through the core of the threads so they are attached to the needle.

4. Loop the threads over the top of the needle and then through the needle again. This should start to make an 'S' shape.

5. Continue looping the threads back and forth, threading through the needle each time so both threads get scrunched onto the length of the needle.

6. When you have reached the ends of both the threads, pull them down the needle until they are resting on the base material surface.

continued on the following page

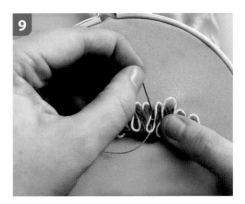

7. You can alter the couched ruffle by pulling the threads out to make a loopy pattern or pushing together to create a tighter ruffle.

8. Anchor the couching by pushing your needle back into the fabric base where you want your ruffle couching to finish.

9. Anchor further by coming up with your needle and going across the embroidery thread, in-between the thread ruffle, making a small straight stitch.

10. You can now experiment with different materials and lengths of thread to create more ruffle couching. It is a versatile and textured stitch.

CHAIN STITCH

Chain stitch is a loop stitch that can be used to create a variety of both organic and geometric patterns. I use it a lot for any floral-based sample ideas or designs, and it works very well as a securing stitch for using with embellishments.

To create a chain stitch you need to use a thread that will easily pull through a base material. Pull a needle and thread through a base and then go back through the base, very close to the first stitch, not pulling the thread tightly so that it is loose on the surface, to create a large loop. The needle and thread should then come up through the base in the centre of that loop to catch it and create the stitch. Once the needle is through the base material in the centre of the thread loop, you can pull the thread to the desired tension.

The trick with chain stitches is that they should not be pulled too tightly if you want them to be curved and soft. Once you have created the first loop stitch, this can be finished by putting your needle back through the base on the outer edge of the loop, to prevent it from pulling out. For a linear chain stitch, you then create your next loop inside the first one and continue the pattern.

Chain stitch linear examples. You can see the way the stitch has been used in a range of directions, using different threads and tensions to create a variety of shapes.

A detailed floral sample with layered chain stitch loops. This is a very buildable stitch that you can layer up by starting with a thicker thread and adding thinner threads on top. This gives dimension and creates a more tactile floral idea.

- You can manipulate the loops of your chain stitch by pulling out a longer length or making them more angular to create geometric patterns and shapes. To create a wider loop, bring your needle through the base further apart from the first stitch, pull this tight and come up inside the loop, then pull to make a triangular-shaped stitch.
- Try using a single looped chain stitch to attach a petal-shaped embellishment for a quick and simple floral idea. I like to embellish these single stitches by adding on a small bead or sequin when my needle and thread is in the middle of the loop, then finishing the stitch as usual to secure.
- Chain stitches as single loops are a great stitch to layer on thicker couched threads or straight stitches to create sunburst patterns and intricate details on samples. Always consider that you can layer stitches on top of stitches for more interest.
- To create a more geometric chain stitch you can create blocked patterns by making a small grid with two chain stitches, and then adding another two so that they cross

over the first two, to make a layered block. This could also be achieved by playing with base material transparency and adding stitches on separate bases that then layer together when stacked.

FRENCH KNOTS

A French knot is a knotted stitch that stands three-dimensionally off the base surface. It is fantastic for creating texture on samples. The stitch is shaped by wrapping a thread around the needle so that it creates a knot as the needle is pulled back through the base material, and catches the loops of thread in a tightly condensed shape.

I like French knots as, although they are often seen as a very delicate and tiny stitch, they can be pulled and manipulated into tactile and sculptural forms. I use French knots for securing 3D embellishments, as the knot that is created also acts as a stopper and prevents embellishments from pulling

French knot samples. You can see the way the stitch has been used in varying scales to change its appearance. It can secure embellishments in place and adds a tactile quality to samples. Other samples show knots that have deliberately not been pulled tight to create loops, to make a more organic and messy stitch for nature-inspired samples.

out of the base material. French knots are best practised with a thicker thread such as a wool, which is helpful when getting used to making the stitch and is more visible. The stitches can be created in a variety of threads, two threads together or act as dotted accents for patterns.

How to Create Giant French Knots
Upping the scale of French knots to the size of a coin or even bigger can give you a really good understanding of how the stitch is formed and worked through. The key with larger

stitched knots is having a good supportive base with widely spaced holes so that you can easily pull your thicker threads through the base. It can take a bit of experimenting with threads and bases to figure out a perfect combination that doesn't hurt your fingers too much to pull through, but the end results are a tactile and chunky textured surface. Once you have got the hang of the stitch, you can also experiment with using your fingers as a sewing needle and wrapping and pulling really chunky threads through bases.

- Large-eyed needle with blunt end (children's plastic needles are great for this).
- Base material with spaced holes, such as: a shower mat, non-slip drawer lining, burlap sack or plastic grid mesh. Larger holes will give you potential for stitching larger knots.
- Selection of thick, chunky threads, such as: ribbons, cut strips of fabric, rope or cord – anything that has flexibility, will curl around into a solid knot shape when manipulated and will pull through the eye of your needle.

1. To secure your thread, create a large knot to prevent it slipping through the base material then come up through one of the holes to start. I secure my base in an embroidery hoop to prevent slipping.

2. Wrap the thread around the needle, so the thread is going away from you, not towards you. Keeping the tension of the thread not overly tight but not too loose on the wraps, wrap the thread around three or four times.

3. When you have wrapped the thread around the needle, pull the needle through the next hole in the base to the back to complete your stitch, easing the wraps over the eye of the needle with your finger.

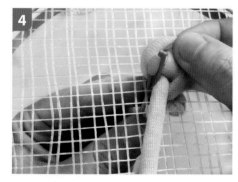

4. If the wraps are tight and you are struggling to pull the needle through, they may need an extra wiggle to get them loose. Alternatively, try working a wrap at a time over the needle eye.

5. Once the needle is pulled through, hold the remaining thread tight until the thread tail goes through the knot, then pull hard. This tension will help to prevent extra loops in your knot that can make it look irregular.

6. Repeat the stitch or trim off and create with another thread. For chunky knots I find it easier to leave the ends loose and then tie off at the end. Mix and match textures for a tactile sample.

CHAPTER 3

PAPER

Paper is a material that is often overlooked within textiles; it is seen as something that only has its uses within other crafts. However, I believe paper is a highly versatile and easily accessible material to both find and use. It is easy to stitch through and can also fold and keep its shape, which opens up many possibilities with 3D and structured embellishments. Paper can be easily coloured by adding paints, inks and other mediums to its surface.

TYPES OF PAPER TO COLLECT

There is a large variety of paper types that you can pair with stitch. Art papers and traditional paper types may be the immediate ones that come to mind, but if you branch out a little there are many different papers that all can be used within a textile setting. I have elaborated on my favourites and some of the more unusual ones are below.

Wallpaper Samples

You can often pick up wallpaper samples from DIY stores. They come in a huge variety of colours, textures and patterns. The best thing about wallpaper is its lovely thickness, which makes it a dream to stitch through as it doesn't tear as easily as some of the thinner paper varieties. I am particularly fond of using lining paper – again, the thickness of this is great and if you add any paint, ink or water-based medium on top it soaks in and gives a soft edge, which is very pleasing. You can

sometimes find discontinued sample books from wallpaper companies within scrapstores, which is even better as you are also recycling.

Text-Based Paper

Using papers with any text can add extra pattern and interest to a project. Recycling and text-based papers go hand in hand, and you can select specifics based on the snippets of text that you want to use and see within a sample. Starting off simply, you may think about old book pages, dress patterns, magazines or newspapers. I have also previously found bundles of vintage handwritten postcards in antique shops. Text-based papers are great for adding sentimental value, whether from a letter, an envelope, a page from a travel journal or a map location.

You do need to be careful when using text to ensure you correctly follow copyright rules, particularly if you are making a project that is not for personal use. Another thing to watch is that some text-based papers are very thin and delicate, which means they need to be gently handled and stitched with as small a needle as possible to reduce tearing.

Paper Packaging

Everyone will have paper packaging around their home or workspace. Although many forms of paper packaging can be recycled fairly easily, you can also reuse it by adding it into a creative project. Food packaging is an obvious one – use items such as egg cartons, cereal boxes and any outer card or paper layer from a food product that is clean. I also enjoy cutting out

Details of 2D stitched paper sequin sample on denim.

barcodes to create fun black-and-white striped papers. Items like used tea bags and coffee filter papers can be used if they are dried and any loose tea leaves or coffee grounds removed. The staining from the tea or coffee can add a vintage quality.

Art or Handmade Papers

Art papers can be the most expensive papers to purchase, depending on the type, but you can get some beautiful textures and colours of paper to play with. I often think of papers that have different surface qualities such as tissue paper, crepe paper, printer paper, or papers with metallic or neon coatings. Handmade papers are beautifully tactile, have lovely edges and can be studded with dried flowers, glitter, fragments of other papers, or swirled with colours and dyes. Again, it is always worth looking in scrapstores for papers like this, as sometimes a local printer or art shop may send over reams of paper with slight imperfections.

Household Recycling

Rummaging through my recycling bin is something I do fairly often, and if I can use something myself I would much rather give it a second lease of life than throw it away. Any sort of cardboard packaging that comes in the post is always great. With brown card you can sometimes peel off the top layer of paper to reveal a corrugated texture underneath. Stiffer cards and papers make great bases for stitching onto, as well as stitching with. Other recycled ideas you may want to think about could involve using make-up or product packaging. A lot of brands go all out with fancy finishes such as flocked paper, metallic paper or laser-cut shapes, all of which can be snipped out and reused in a creative way. The garden or garage is another place to find materials and inspiration – old seed packets can be great to reuse.

Selection of collected papers including wallpaper, vintage postcards, paper packaging, art papers and household recycling. See the difference in patterns, colours and finishes of paper.

STITCHING ONTO PAPER AS A BASE

Paper is a good material to use to start being more experimental with your mixed media journey, and I think it is great to use as a base instead of fabric. This can open up many possibilities for making stitched cards, collages or paintings. You don't need to use an embroidery hoop to stitch with paper as is much stiffer than many types of fabric. The flipside of that is, because of paper's structure and composition, once you have punched a hole in it with a needle, it is there to stay. You have to be precise about where you want your needle to puncture the paper.

A great exercise to begin experimenting with paper and stitch is to draw some simple shapes or lines onto a piece of card or paper – I would recommend something fairly thick, such as thin cardboard or wallpaper. Then go over your drawn shapes with a needle and thread. Keep your stitches simple to start with and only use a straight stitch. Make sure you tie a large knot at the end of your thread to ensure it doesn't rip through the paper. Always use a small needle when working with a paper base to avoid having large holes, as this can cause an issue with thread pulling through. Think of your paper base in the same way as fabric and treat it as such.

TIPS AND TRICKS FOR USING PAPER AS A BASE

- Create a collage of papers first by gluing different papers together like a patchwork quilt and then stitching through the collage with a needle and thread. To add texture, try using different thicknesses of thread as different weights of line on the paper surface.
- Try your hand with your favourite embroidery stitches, stitched onto paper. Some stitches may be easier or harder to do, but it will give you a new version of how you could potentially change certain stitches to suit different base mediums.
- Add paint or colour to your base paper first – this could be very abstract splashes and shapes of colour that can be enhanced further with stitch. Think of your patterns giving you a blueprint of where to add your stitches on top of the surface.
- If you find the paper difficult to pull your needle through, you can always add a small piece of masking tape to the end of your finger for extra grip to pull through the needle.

A stitched paper sample with simple embroidery details. The background was an old piece of painted paper taken from a sketchbook.

USING PAPER TO CREATE 2D EMBELLISHMENTS

I am a big believer that there is no single way to try a technique or idea, and every person will have a different variation. The ideas I will include below are a taster of some of the ways that I create 2D paper embellishments. Add your own twists and ideas into the mix to make the techniques your own.

As well as using paper as the base material, we can also create our own flat paper shapes, sequins and embellishments and add these onto bases with stitch. You can easily cut out paper shapes using craft punches or by cutting freehand with scissors. You may want to consider ripping out some shapes to get that lovely torn edge that can add an organic texture – this can look great with handmade papers. Craft punches come in a variety of sizes, shapes and styles, and the common office-style hole punch can create small usable sequins.

I always begin any project by cutting out my shapes and embellishments from different papers so I have a selection of shapes, textures and colours to work with. Don't throw away the offcuts as these negative shapes can also come in handy, either for stencils or for using as layering pieces for other samples. Treat your paper embellishments as you would any other embellishment or sequin. I like to stitch paper shapes onto fabric by pushing my needle through the centre of the shape, making a small straight stitch and then pushing my needle back through the shape and the base to the other side. I don't worry too much about stitching all around the edges of the shapes. If you just add a small straight stitch through the paper embellishment centre, this gives you options for layering and tucking details underneath the shapes you have already stitched down. Stitches can be added around each paper embellishment for added pattern too.

You can also think about layering multiple shapes on one thread. Pull your needle through your base, then thread on your largest shape first. Add another smaller shape, then another and another, before putting your needle back through the base to create a stacked or layered embellishment. This is a great way to create a speedy sample, as there are fewer stitches but more layers and embellishments added to your fabric.

Examples of different-shaped craft punches and hole punches. These punches will also work with other mixed media materials.

Flat paper embellishments stacked and layered across a denim base. The vintage postcard sequins allow words to be selected and add sentiment to the sample.

How to Create Foiled Paper Sequins

This is a simple technique using paper, double-sided tape and textile foils to create your own metallic patterned sequin sheet. The sheets can be made in any patterns or colours you wish and then easily chopped up using a punch or scissors into sequin embellishments to add to your sample.

MATERIALS NEEDED

- Any sort of paper or thin card – something with a smooth surface such as gift wrap, sugar paper or coloured printer paper.
- Double-sided tape.
- Glue dots (optional).
- Textile foils – thin metallic foils that are often used within textile printing but are great for adding to embellishments.
- Metal spoon.
- Aluminium foil tape (you can find this in most DIY stores).
- Scissors.
- Craft punch/hole punch (optional).

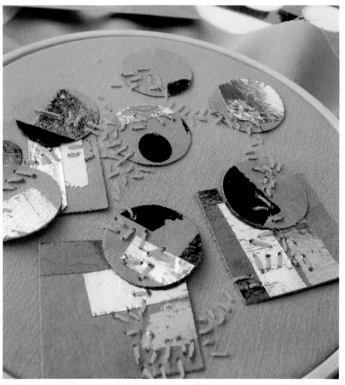

A finished sheet of foiled paper sequins and the finished punched-out embellishments stitched onto a fabric base.

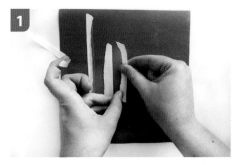

1. Begin by tearing or cutting double-sided tape to create stripes or any sort of pattern on the paper or thin card. I often tear double-sided tape as it can gum up scissors when used.

2. If you are using glue dots to make circular shapes you can also add these onto your paper. It is helpful to think of your pattern as abstractly as possible, rather than trying to create a picture.

3. Peel the paper off your first tape stripe and add a piece of textile foil directly onto the sticky side. The textile foil always needs to be placed with the silver side down onto the sticky side and the coloured side up.

continued on the following page

4. Give the textile foil a rub with the back of a metal spoon or a piece of card to ensure it sticks to every bit of your double-sided tape. Then gently unpeel to reveal your metallic stripe underneath.

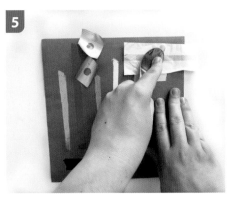

5. Continue peeling back the paper from the double-sided tape and adding the textile foils to create a colourful, metallic pattern across the paper. You can mix foil colours or keep to a single colour, depending on your project.

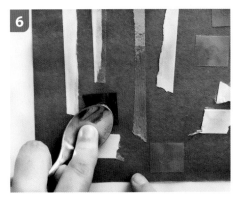

6. If using glue dots, add your textile foil to these in the same way as the tape, rub with a spoon to ensure the edges are stuck, then unpeel. The glue dots will create a circular shape, rather than stripes.

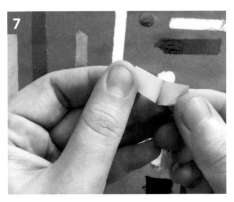

7. When your foils are fully transferred onto your tape you can add extra details by using aluminium foil tape. Apply the foil tape by cutting or tearing, then peel the edge of the backing paper and stick to your background.

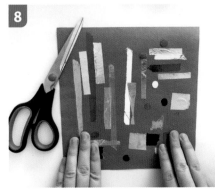

8. Continue building your shapes with foil tape to complete your abstract pattern. You can layer the foils on top of the metallic stripes and dots already created or you can add the foil directly to the paper as separate patterns.

9. Once you are happy with your metallic pattern, you can cut your sequins either using a craft punch or scissors. These sequins can then be stitched onto your fabric or paper base to create some exciting metallic samples.

USING PAPER TO CREATE 3D EMBELLISHMENTS

Paper is a fantastic material for 3D shapes and embellishments because of its ability to hold its structure. One of the best ways to experiment and play with this idea is to cut or punch different paper shapes from various paper sources and manipulate the paper, looking at different ways and combinations in which it can be folded, scrunched, pleated or twisted to create a pop-up shape. Then see how you can stitch that shape onto your base. It is important to add a stitch that will support the embellishment when stitching on very 3D shapes so they won't be squashed flat.

I sometimes look at how I can add a 3D embellishment into something else that can provide this support, such as another more solid embellishment, or creating stitched clusters of 3D paper embellishments that support each other. The idea of clustering them together will help to create tension and rigidity so that they cannot pull out of shape. Some papers will also work better than others for creating 3D structures; I have found wallpaper can have too much of a fabric quality and, while it is able to be folded, it does not create that clean, crisp, sharp fold that is needed for creating very structured embellishments. Thinner papers and more rigid paper or card are often ideal, such as pages of old books, printer paper or cardboard packaging to name a few.

Paper Twisted Ropes

Cut a long strip of thin paper, such as a magazine page, coloured A4 or even tissue paper. Twist the paper into a long thin rope, as long or short as you wish. You will find differences with the tightness of the twist and the way the twist stays together as you experiment with papers. Don't worry if you get some small tears or breaks in the paper as you twist; this can add texture to the finished rope. The finished twist could incorporate different coloured papers and can be stitched onto fabric almost like a cord. I would attach it by couching over the twisted paper rope with my thread, looping and twisting the rope across the base so that it stands up from the surface.

Paper ropes created using crepe paper streamers. The thin paper twists tightly and gives an almost corded quality.

Details of mixed papers for creating three-dimensional embellishment ideas.

Paper Curls

As well as being very structured and sharp to create angular shapes, you can also create some soft, curled and looped shapes with paper. Experiment with cutting various widths of paper – any thickness or type is great for this, apart from card. Curl the paper strip around a cylindrical object such as a pen or your finger, and then stitch onto fabric by putting a small straight stitch through one end of the paper shape so the top of the loop or curl is free from the base. You can enhance the loops so they stand upright on the surface or play with smaller curls of paper, which would make a great textural surface and could be layered with several curls and colours of paper. This technique is very effective with painted or patterned paper types.

Pleated Paper Fans

Pleating or folding paper back and forth onto itself to make a concertina can create some fun 3D effects. You can play with pleating different shapes, such as squares of paper, folding even sections back and forth to create zigzag shapes. I would recommend trying this idea with a thin paper that holds a crease well, such as a coloured A4, recycled packaging or thin card.

When stitching down a pleated paper embellishment, use a simple straight stitch and add the stitches along the bottom of the pleats so the top sections do not get squashed.

For a more floral-inspired pleated embellishment, try cutting semicircles or fan shapes and pleating from the bottom of the shape. When stitching these into position, I push my needle through the end of the pleated shape so the stitch runs through the whole embellishment at the thinnest end, from left to right and then back into the base material. This will mean the pleated shape is attached from one end only to give an organic look.

Curls of paper looped into spirals, which look like ocean waves on this sample.

Pleated paper fans creating a graphic floral sample. The use of recycled envelopes and painted sketchbook papers adds contrast and pattern.

Folded Paper Vessels

This structured technique creates a more geometric outcome and needs a stiff paper. Use something that you can really press a crease into, such as a brown paper bag, seed packet or recycled gift wrap. Get a square of paper, large enough to sit in the palm of your hand, and fold each corner into the centre of the square to create a diamond shape. Then fold this shape in half horizontally and push the left and right edges inwards with your finger to create a triangle shape. This should pop out into a 3D vessel or pyramid shape, which you could stitch onto a base, either way up. When you have the paper folded into position, you can experiment with cutting shapes or snipping a hole into the centre to make different shapes and patterns. These vessels can be scaled up or down with many sorts of paper, stacked and layered to create a repeat pattern.

Folded paper vessels creating a geometric sample. The shapes have been stacked and flipped to interlock and create height.

Flat lay details of three-dimensional paper samples, including pleats, curls, folds and twisted papers.

CHAPTER 4

FABRIC

Fabric and stitch go together hand in hand, and using textiles can be an expected pairing. However, that does not mean that using fabric within your mixed media journey has to be boring. In fact, like with other media, there is an exciting range of fabrics to explore as well as many creative ways in which they can applied and used. Fabric can provide a softer, more organic and flowing result for embellishments and can be manipulated in many ways with stitch and other materials. Stitching through fabric is very easy and therefore is a good beginner option for starting out and exploring different stitches.

TYPES OF FABRIC TO COLLECT

Every textiles enthusiast will have a box – or multiple boxes – somewhere in their home, filled to the brim with fabrics. Some are bought especially for a project idea; others you buy as you like the colour, texture or print; or there are those fabrics that are so precious you are scared of chopping them and using them. Creating embellishments using fabric is a fantastic way to use scraps and small offcuts from precious fabrics that you don't want to bin. It leads into a familiar way to use embellishments from a textile perspective that can build confidence for other more unusual mixed media ideas. Although some fabrics can be quite expensive to purchase, I will go through options and ideas for finding fabrics at low price points. Fabrics all have a beautiful tactile quality; it was that tactility that first drew me towards textile art, and because of that I do find it is easier to shop for fabrics in person rather than online. Fabric shopping is a texture and touch sensory experience.

Natural Fabrics

Natural fabrics are lovely to stitch through as they often have a nice weave structure, which allows thicker threads to pass through the fabric and gives them a stiffness rather than any stretch. This also means they will fray when cut. When looking at natural fabrics, there is a huge variation – think of wool, silk, cotton, denim, hessian or linen. Many dressmaking fabrics that are lighter in weight, as well as heavier-weight interior and upholstery fabrics, have a natural fibre composition. I particularly enjoy stitching onto heavyweight natural fabric bases, as the weave structure and dense fabric give more stability, meaning that my embellishments are going to be supported.

Many pure natural fabrics will be expensive, particularly silks, wools or linen types. Natural fabrics, especially cottons, are very straightforward to dye or colour – most shop-bought dyes are suitable for cotton fabrics. You don't have to use brand-new natural fabrics, and sourcing secondhand or recycled fabrics to work with can lead to some exciting discoveries. Bedding and blankets from secondhand shops are often 100 per cent cotton and nice and thick for stitching with, as well as being a sustainable and pocket-friendly approach. It is also worth a rummage for large tablecloths, tea towels or any clothing. To check the fabric composition, look at the tags on items and you will find a treasure trove of fabrics that can easily be repurposed.

Detail of 3D floral embellishments, pinched and layered to create petals.

Synthetic Fabrics

Synthetic fabric can be found in an exhilarating array of bright colours and metallics of varying transparencies and elasticities. They make great bases for textile samples or for embellishment use and are often a more pocket-friendly version of pure natural fabrics. You can often find mixed synthetics or synthetic versions of silks and wools if you are very conscious of using animal products. A lot of very specialist fabrics are often synthetic, so think along the lines of fabrics with unique properties such as for dancewear, outdoor pursuits or the construction industry. This way you can find fabrics that have stretch, metallic accents, neon flashes or waterproof properties.

The majority of the time, I choose a fabric based on its colours, the way it folds or stretches and how that will link in with my textile and mixed media project. Alternatively, and very simply, you choose a fabric based on whether you like it or not! Synthetics can be tricky to dye, so it is easier to buy them in the colour that you wish to use.

One of my favourite reasons to use synthetic fabrics is because they don't often fray, as many do not have a traditional weave structure. This is particularly great when cutting any embellishments out, as you can chop away with your scissors and your shapes will stay pristine and sharp. If you are concerned about synthetic fabrics and plastic content, look to only purchase synthetic fabrics that are waste, dead-stock or recycled. This keeps them out of landfill and gives them a second use.

Recycled and Scrap Fabrics

These are my favourite sorts of fabrics and can encompass both natural and synthetics, but with the knowledge that you are making the most eco-friendly choice. You can start by looking through your own wardrobe and selecting pieces that are damaged or stained – maybe it's a dress that is too small or a tablecloth handed down from a relative. Spend an afternoon cutting items into fabric squares or panels – this will help to give more of a material feel to the pieces rather than thinking of them as the items they used to be. Recycling your own fabrics is a nice touch of sentimentality, such as keeping a handwritten label or clothing item with personal memories attached. It is also great to have a box of small scraps and offcuts to dive into.

Looking into dead-stock bolt ends of fabrics and old fabric swatches or sample books is another option, as mentioned in Sources for Mixed Media Materials in Chapter 1. Many dead-stock options can be found within scrapstores as well as in specialist online shops. Bolt ends often have the selvedge of a fabric, which can be a lovely detail or feature to use. Old swatch books from carpet companies or furniture designers will often include mini squares of fabrics in various colour-ways – these are a perfect size for snipping out and using as embellishments. Sometimes swatch book fabrics have a glued paper backing on them. This can either be ironed or peeled off, or just ignore it, cut it up and use the fabrics as normal.

Unusual Fabrics

Fabric is a looser term here, as I describe materials to collect that have the functions of fabric, such as a woven structure or soft, easily stitched surface. Items such as sponges, foam sheets, ribbons and trims can all be used effectively. Sponges are very fun to use – think of all the colours and variations: dish sponges, make-up sponges or natural sponges. They can be sliced and chopped into shapes and provide 3D elements because of their depth and soft texture that can be compressed

A selection of fabric embellishments using foam, sponges and felt. The sliced circles are created using foam hair rollers.

or puffed out. I also like to collect hair rollers – those that come in long foam tubes, where you can remove the wire centre and slice the remaining foam into discs to stitch with. Ribbons and trims can be pleated and layered to create lots of texture – they can be used as a fabric base as well as a thread idea, as explored in Chapter 2.

ADDING PAINT TO FABRIC TO CHANGE THE PROPERTIES

Most fabric by design is soft, pliable, and folds and drapes very easily, which is why it is such a popular choice for textile projects. However, when looking more closely into creative embellishments and using fabric as a medium, this can sometimes be a hindrance. Soft, floppy fabrics are more difficult to cut out with craft punches to create your own sequins and they can also fray very easily.

One of my favourite ways to help with this is to look at changing the fabric property by making it a stiffer, crisper surface that will go through a punch or can be cut more easily with scissors. You can do this by adding a layer of paint to your fabric, which you can apply with a brush or a sponge – or just splash it on! When the paint has dried, see how much the fabric surface has changed and if it feels crisper. If it still feels quite soft, you can build up the paint layers bit by bit. When you feel the fabric is crisp enough, try punching a shape with your hole punch or craft punch, or cut with scissors for a fray-free embellishment.

Examples of painted lace. Painting the fabric has given it stiffness, allowing it to be punched cleanly with a shaped craft punch to make small square sequins.

- Experiment with different sorts of paints, watering them down to achieve a thinner consistency that will soak into the fabric fibres. I prefer to use acrylic or household emulsion. The paint doesn't need to be expensive or branded – any make will do.
- This is also a great way to change the colour of your fabric or add some pattern or flecks of additional colour to a base, to create a patterned background to stitch onto.
- Finer and lighter fabrics will work better with this technique than anything too thick or chunky. The fabric needs to be thin enough to pass under a punch.
- Try painting sheer and lace fabrics and mesh, laying the fabric onto a paper sheet to catch paint residue that can be repurposed into another material sheet.
- It is a good idea to try punching smaller shapes first, such as using an office-style hole punch. If this works, you can then try using a larger shaped punch.
- If the fabric is still not punching out cleanly, you can try a smaller craft punch or add more paint. Some fabrics will still need cutting with scissors, but will have a cleaner cut edge.
- When stitching the painted fabric as an embellishment, it will be stiffer to push a needle through, but it should not be too difficult. Make sure you wait until the fabric is completely dry to avoid getting wet paint on your needle.

LAYERING FABRICS WITH 2D TACTILE BACKGROUNDS

You can use any fabric as a background for stitching a mixed media sample, whether a single piece of fabric or experimenting with layering fabrics together. There are no rules on how you can layer or stack your fabrics to create a more interesting background to work onto. This can give you some ideas for the patterns and colours with your embellishments and stitching. I often layer fabrics – it can be helpful with colour mixing, adding texture and pattern, and generally giving more interest to a sample idea. I have several tips and tricks that I use to create layered backgrounds that you can incorporate into your own mixed media journey.

Playing with Opacity

Many fine fabrics such as organza, mesh or lace, which are interesting surfaces to work onto, can be difficult to stitch as they are very lightweight and not very supportive bases. This means lots of embellishment detail can weigh down or even fall off when applied. Layering a heavier-weight fabric, such as a denim, cotton canvas or linen, with your lightweight fabric on top, and then stitching through both layers together gives you the texture and pattern of the finer fabric with the stability of the heavier fabric behind. You could even play with trapping details within the bottom layer, so you have glimpses of different embellishments peeking through the layers of fabric.

A layered fabric sample with an opaque dark fabric base and mesh overlay. Threads have been trapped in-between the base and layers of mesh, almost like confetti. This gives an illusion of depth and a 3D nature.

FABRIC PATCHWORK

Treat your base material as a patchwork quilt, and fold, cut and layer different snippets of other fabrics together, pinning down to secure. I would recommend having one large piece as a foundation base with smaller stripes, shapes and snippets on top of this solid layer. To help to secure your background patchwork, put all the layers together into an embroidery hoop before you begin stitching.

My tip for trying this technique is to treat the patched fabrics as one solid background, and work over them with your stitches and embellishments without worrying about stitching around every patch. The more stitches and embellishments are added on top of your handstitched fabric patchwork, the more secure your background will become. You can always use pins or small straight stitches to secure your patches in place first if they are moving around.

A patchwork fabric sample. You can see how the embroidery hoop is used to trap the edges of the patchwork shapes and small straight stitches have been scattered across the pieces of fabric to secure and add pattern to the sample.

Cutaway and Appliqué Details

You may think of cutaway detail being used within machine stitch ideas, but it is also a nice technique to try with hand stitching. I find it easier to cut away from the front of your fabric base, which means anything slightly messy can be on the fabric back. Try cutting some patches of light fabric, such as organza, netting or fine silk in a sharp contrasting colour, and pin to the back of your fabric base. On the front of the fabric you can create the cutaway shape. I tend to keep the shape simple, such as a square or a wonky circle. Draw the shape with a pen on the front, making sure your whole shape is within the patch of fabric pinned to the back. Then you can stitch around the shape using a solid stitch that has no breaks, such

as a straight stitch, with each stitch being very close together. Carefully part the top and bottom layer of fabric and cut the top-layer fabric away within the stitched edges. This reveals the second base fabric and appliqué through the cutaway.

Colour Mixing

Layering of fabrics can help with colour mixing or pulling out and drawing back different tones and shades. If I am working with a fabric that is very bright and zingy, particularly anything neon, sometimes it can be a little too much on the eyes. If that is the case, adding a layer of fine, transparent fabric in a very neutral colour on top of the bright fabric will help tone down that zing and make it a lot more aesthetically pleasing. This will also work in the opposite way; if a colour needs brightening up – maybe a dull green or navy that needs a pop – I can add a layer of fine fabric, perhaps in the same tones but more jewel-like or something with flecks of metallic or a texture that adds interest, to enhance the colours and tones.

3D FABRIC EMBELLISHMENT TECHNIQUES

Fabric is a great choice for creating your own mixed media embellishments as it can be manipulated in different ways to create tactile, 3D shapes that add depth to a sample idea. The general properties of most fabrics are that they are a lot softer and more flowing than using paper, so any 3D shapes we try to create will have those features. Think along the lines of a soft fold or rolled edge rather than something very crisp and sharp. This lends well to creating embellishments that reflect organic forms such as florals. The word manipulation is key, as with creating 3D embellishments it is considering how you can manipulate your fabric in different ways to achieve varied shapes, as well as stretching the possibilities and properties of your fabric to create an embellishment. Although you can manipulate your fabric using the same methods as with paper, the results will be very different because of the material properties.

A fabric sample with layered cutaway appliqué detail. Here the patches of fabric have been placed on both the front and reverse of the base fabric. The reverse cutaway has a sharp edge and a stained glass appearance with the fabric peeking through.

A selection of pre-cut sequins from a mix of fabrics. I like to cut lots of simple shapes such as squares, circles and rectangles as these are the easiest to manipulate and work with all of the techniques in this chapter. These shapes have been cut freehand with scissors, a craft punch and a die-cutter.

Fabric can be cut into embellishments using scissors, a manual die-cutter or craft punches (if you have a stiffer fabric such as a leatherette or coated material). For the 3D techniques explained below, I have cut my fabric shapes with a pair of scissors, as this gives me the ability to create more unique and organic shapes. You can often fold a thinner fabric and cut multiple shapes at once, keeping spares in a specific box for ready-to-use embellishments or fabric sequins. A great sample exercise is to get a base fabric in an embroidery hoop, and then trial different techniques using different fabrics, either pre-cut into shapes or cutting as you go along.

How to Create Fabric Sequin Stacks

This fun technique is a great one for creating towers and vertical 3D shapes using sliced foam circles to add depth and texture. The sequin stacks can be adapted with different fabrics, shapes, colours and the height of the stacks. This works very well with using foam-type fabric or anything with some depth and sponginess, such as neoprene, thick felt, knit or jersey. The lightness of foam also helps to give you more scope to create taller stacks.

MATERIALS NEEDED

- Foam hair rollers (wire insides removed) or spongy fabric, cut into 1–2cm (½–¾in) circles.
- Fabric base – something sturdy such as thick felt, calico or cotton canvas.
- Long sewing needle with a sharp point.
- Scissors.
- Embroidery thread – any sort.
- Small beads or paper straws with small hole – any colour to suit your sample.
- Embroidery hoop – any size to fit your fabric base securely.

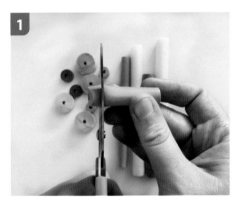

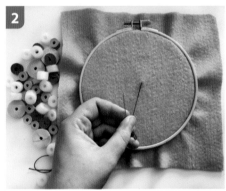

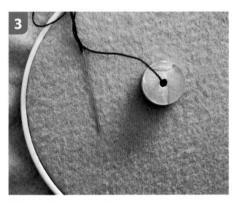

1. Cut your foam hair rollers into rounds, roughly 1–2cm (½–¾in) in thickness, making sure you have removed the wire from inside the roller first.

2. Put your base fabric into your embroidery hoop, making sure the fabric is nice and tight, then pull through your needle and embroidery thread with knotted end.

3. To start the stack, stitch on your first foam circle embellishment, pulling the foam circle down the thread so it is flat on the fabric base.

4. Add something small onto your thread, such as a bead. Alternatively you can cut a small piece of paper straw and thread it onto your foam circle.

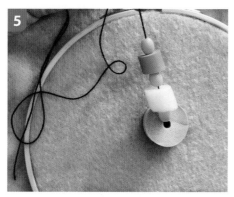

5. Keep adding alternate pieces of sliced foam circle and small beads on your thread until you are happy with your stack height. Finish the stack with a bead as your stopper.

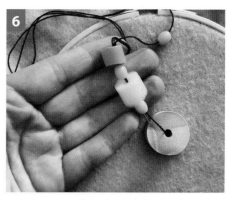

6. Push your needle back through every layer of your stack, apart from your stopper – this can be a little fiddly. Then pull the thread tight to pull the embellishments vertically.

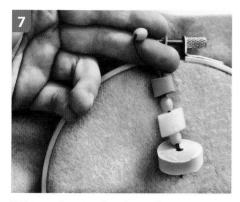

7. You may have to adjust the tension on your embroidery thread to ensure your sequin stack is the same tension throughout the layers, and there are no loops.

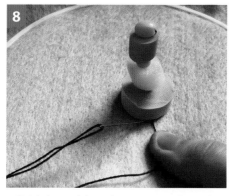

8. Finish the stack by making a very small straight stitch next to your completed stack. This helps to secure the tension of the thread, preventing a wobbly stack.

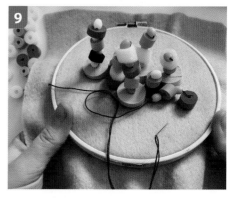

9. Repeat the steps to create more stacks. Play with height, colours and patterns within the stacks. If any stacks are wobbly, stitch through them again to add tension and give extra structure.

Rolled fabric sequin idea, experimenting with stacking rolls of fabric to build the surface. The contrast of the neon cotton and grey felt gives the sample zing and interest.

Rolled Fabric Sequins

This technique works well with strips of fabric. Most varieties will work, especially slightly thicker fabrics such as leatherette, canvas or felt, or you can try with thinner fabrics to create softer rolls. To create a hollow circle that sits on your fabric, simply roll the edges of your preferred shape to create a circle and then stitch the inner edge of the roll to your fabric surface with a straight stitch, so that the top is three-dimensional and free.

- You can secure your rolled fabric sequin vertically or horizontally onto your base. To secure horizontally, add a straight stitch at each side of your roll.
- For a different shape, cut a circle and roll from the edge (as opposed to the middle) to create a more pointed cone shape. This is a great one for a petal-type embellishment.
- If your fabric is denser and holds its shape well, you can stitch further rolls on top of other rolls to stack them off the base.
- Experiment with layering up the rolled fabric sequins, criss-crossed on top of each other on the base, to create geometric patterns.

Fabric Loops

This technique works well with slightly thicker non-fraying fabrics, such as scuba, neoprene, velvet or foam sheets, which will stand up off the base when folded. Cut a long, thin rectangle of fabric, the width of your thumbnail or narrower. Fold in half and cut all the way down the length of the rectangle from the folded edge, but don't cut through the bottom. Unfold the rectangle and then loop the ends of the fabric together to create a 3D embellishment – experiment with looping under and over to create different effects. Stitch onto your fabric base from the two end pieces, with a small straight stitch through both ends, and back into the base.

- Layer the fabric loops together to create dense, ruffled areas with smaller loops stacked onto longer loops.
- Fabrics with two different sides will look effective with this technique, as when looping you glimpse both the front and back of the fabric.

- Loops can also hang over the edges of bases as they are only attached from the end. This can give an organic feel to a sample.
- This technique works well when the stitched end is tucked around a central circular embellishment to create a motif design.

Looped fabric sample idea, using mixed leatherette and velvet 3D loops, which retain their shape and structure. This motif idea can be layered up with other techniques and materials.

Folded Fabric Scales

This technique works well with any sort of fabric, using regular shapes such as squares or circles. Thinner fabrics, such as lace, mesh, cotton or silk, will create a flatter and smoother fabric scale, while thicker, chunky fabrics, such as suede, upholstery canvas or foam sheets, will create a dense, spongy fabric scale. Fold your fabric embellishments into any shape you wish and stitch down with a straight stitch through the centre of the shapes.

Scaled fabric sample. The folded scales tessellate as you tuck them closely together with no gaps, to create an interlocking pattern. You can see how some fabric scales have been layered with multiple fabrics to add more detail to the sample.

- This is a great technique for creating a scaled texture, which can be achieved by folding fabric circle embellishments in half and securing with a small straight stitch in the centre. Add the next folded scale so it tucks under the first.
- Layering smaller shapes on top of larger ones and then folding as one embellishment is a quick way to create multicoloured patterns.
- Try folding your shapes into quarters and stitching. The placement of your securing stitch will affect how three-dimensional your embellishments will become.
- This technique can create repeat patterns that can be stitched over a large surface by repeating your shapes and folds.

Pinched Fabric Embellishments

This technique works well with thin fabrics, such as silk, crochet doilies, printed polycotton or lace. Cut shapes such as freeform wonky circles or elongated oval shapes for floral ideas. Pinch your fabric embellishment in half from the base of the shape, then fold back the edges to create a pinched 3D shape. Stitch in place on your base by pushing your needle and thread through all of the pinched folds with a horizontal straight stitch, and then straight into the base with a small straight stitch.

- To create a pasta bow-type shape, use a circle and push your needle through the centre, moving in and out to make small pinched folds. Pull hard when the needle is through to ruffle the embellishment into a bow shape.
- For floral ideas and motifs, cutting a different shape for each pinched embellishment creates a more organic look. You can also snip the edges of the embellishments when stitched into place for a fluttered edge.
- Layering opaque fabrics with fine or light materials can make it easier to see the pinched effect and build up surface detail.
- Experiment with layering up various pinched fabric embellishments in clusters across a fabric base to make your own motifs.

Pinched fabric sample. This shows variations of manipulating different fabrics to construct a 3D floral idea. This can be layered and built up with softer- and heavier-weight fabrics. Some edges have been snipped to create softness.

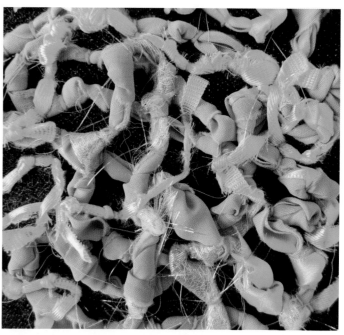

Knotted fabric sample. This multicolour knot embellishment uses a sheer, opaque fabric to give an illusion of shimmer. The knotted strips have been curled and stitched into shape, rather than in lines, to give the sample more texture.

Knotted Fabric Strips

This technique works well with thinner fabrics, such as polycottons, silks, laces and organzas, which can be knotted and pulled into shapes. Simply cut or tear a long strip of fabric and knot along the length to create a 3D textured rope. This knotted fabric rope can then be couched or straight stitched into place on your base.

- You could try knotting two different fabrics together to create multicoloured knotted ropes.

- When attaching the knotted fabrics to your base, think about whether you want to wiggle the knotted embellishments or lay them in a straight line to create different patterns.
- Fraying fabrics work well for this technique, as when knotted the frayed fabric ends create a softer, more flowing texture than a thick solid line.
- Experiment with stitching into the finished knots, when secured, with small beads or sequins to embellish them further.

CHAPTER 5

METAL

Metal is often seen as a very hard, industrial-style material, which perhaps contrasts against the softness that is viewed with mixed media and stitch. Metal provides an interesting juxtaposition that can work very well and can be used to add a contemporary look and feel to your stitched samples and projects. I really enjoy the metallic colours, which immediately add a bit of shine to an embellishment. There are many different types of metals that you can use, some being a little more unusual than others. I think metal can provide structure and weight as an embellishment, and can be treated, in some forms, in the same way as paper.

TYPES OF METAL TO COLLECT

When you think of metal you most likely envisage a solid lump of industrial metal – a material that seems very out of place when used as an embellishment. However, when you open up your ideas a little further, there are many varieties of metal that can be stitched in the same way as you would use a fabric or piece of paper to create an embellishment idea. Metal has great possibilities for recycling and reusing pre-existing materials and items that you can find around your home. It is also possible to colour some metals, so you can get creative with colours and textures too.

Household Recycling

There is more metal in your recycling bin than you probably realise; items such as foil lids from desserts or yoghurt pots, metal coffee pods, tinfoil, drinks cans and ring pulls. Reusing metal is an inexpensive way to add new materials into your sampling. Metal needs to be washed and cleaned before use to ensure it is safe to use.

One of my favourite recycled metals to use are tomato paste tubes, which are mostly metal. You need to be very careful when cutting them open, as the edges are extremely sharp. I tend to snip off the top and bottom of the tube with a pair of scissors, then carefully slide the scissors up one edge and open it out into a flat sheet. The remaining tomato paste can be washed off and the metal is then ready to use. Different brands of tomato paste have slightly different coloured metals, so you can build up a nice collection. Metal coffee pods also need to be carefully cut open, flattened and rinsed. These come in a great range of colours so you can get a metallic rainbow.

Detail of rolled metal vessels constructed with recycled tomato paste tubes. These shapes look like coral forms.

Examples of washed, cut-out sheets of recycled metal from flattened tomato paste tubes and foil lids, as well as small metal washers. You can see the vast array of metal colours, from thin silver foils to thicker gold and copper sheets from the tomato paste tubes.

Art Foil

A slightly more expensive option is to buy ready-cut sheets of art foil. These metal sheets come in a range of colours, metal types and sizes. Art foil is very thin and flexible, and is great for manipulating into a range of structured and three-dimensional shapes for creating embellishments. Art foil is very easy to cut into shapes using craft punches or hole punches.

DIY Materials

Exploring your shed or garage can turn out a lot of interesting embellishments that are ready to use. One of my favourite embellishments of all is the simple washer. You can get washers that are made of materials other than metal, but they come in a huge range of sizes, shapes and thicknesses; some washers are so small and delicate they already look like fancy sequins.

Examples of collected metal embellishments that have been painted with acrylic and spray paint. The patterns have been made using stencils, other fabrics and masking tape.

Metal Wire

Wire is a fantastically versatile material; one of the biggest benefits of it being its ability to sculpt and bend into self-supporting shapes and patterns. I always have a variety of wires available to use, which include jewellery wire, plant or garden wire and wired cables. I use wire a lot as an unconventional thread idea (as mentioned in Chapter 2), but it also has benefits as an embellishment material.

It is easiest to start with a wire that is fairly thin and easy to bend and manipulate with your fingers. Jewellery wire is great for this as you can buy it in a range of gauges, colours and finishes. Plant wire can be picked up from garden centres and is very inexpensive; it can come with a green plastic coating on the outside or as plain silver metal. You will need a pair of pliers or wire snips to cut any wire as it very quickly blunts sharp scissors. Wire is very easy to stitch onto fabric as it can be attached by couching.

EMBOSSED METAL 2D SEQUINS

You can cleanly cut any sort of thin sheet metal, such as art foil, tinfoil or flattened metal tubes, to create different 2D embellishments to stitch onto a base. Unlike fabric, thin sheet metal is really easy to punch out into embellishment shapes using a craft punch or hole punch. These sheets can be further adorned with detail before being cut into shapes by embossing the metal with a pointed implement, such as a pencil or the end of a ballpoint pen.

Embossing is a way of adding decorative pattern onto a malleable surface. You can draw and doodle, and rather than the pattern appearing as a drawn line it is pressed into the surface to create a raised line on one side of the metal and an indented line on the other side. This can give endless opportunity for adding decorative patterns, doodles, text and drawings onto your embellishments.

Consider other DIY fixings, such as nuts, bolts, hooks, cogs, brackets and old car or watch components. I look for anything that has a pre-existing hole in it, which means I will be able to easily stitch the embellishment onto a base. You can use rusted washers as well as very shiny and new ones; rusted washers can always be treated or painted before use to ensure there is no rust transfer. Adding paint to washers can give a colourful patterned appearance to add interest to a project. One thing to be aware of is that having a textile base with lots of metal washers stitched on is going to create a very heavy sample and this will alter the drape of the base underneath.

EMBOSSING METAL: TIPS AND TRICKS

- Embossed marks and patterns work best with a flat sheet of metal with no ripples or marks. I would recommend rolling your metal flat with a rolling pin before starting to get an even, thin layer to work into.
- Try playing with different implements to create various marks on your metal sheets; you could experiment using the prongs of a fork, the end of a nail or even a knitting needle.
- It is easier to emboss your pattern onto your metal sheet as a whole piece, then cut or punch it into embellishment shapes.
- If your embossed line is very faint, you may need to go over it again, pressing harder into the surface. It can help to rest on something such as a pad of paper when you do this.

- Another way to add an embossed pattern is to use a very thin metal such as tinfoil. Add a textured stencil or fabric such as lace underneath the tinfoil and then carefully roll over the foil with a rolling pin or put it through a pasta machine to emboss the texture. This is a similar technique to doing a wax crayon rub through paper to achieve a pattern.
- Explore whether you want to use the embossed metal with raised or indented lines to create different textured sequins.
- To easily poke a hole into your punched embellishments to attach onto bases, secure the metal sequin to a piece of sticky tack and push a tapestry needle into the sequin.

Embossed metal examples. I have used various textures including lace, zigzag stencils and old components from machinery to create the different patterns, as well as doodling into the metal sheet with an old paintbrush.

Stitched sample showing finished embossed metal sequins that have been cut with a shaped craft punch and stitched flat onto a fabric background with a small straight stitch. The result is a very lightweight, shiny, metallic sequin. The sample could be built further with 3D metal embellishment ideas.

3D METAL EMBELLISHMENT TECHNIQUES

As with paper, metal as a material can hold its structure much better than fabric and so it has lots of opportunity to create interesting 3D shapes. Metal can often be much stiffer to work with than paper but it is more hardwearing. Again, it is about experimenting with manipulation, seeing how you can fold, ripple, scrunch or pinch the metal to create a new shape – there is no wrong way to do it! I have shared below some of my favourite ways to create 3D metal sequins and embellishments to make the most from this great material.

Rolled Metal Vessels

You can create your own 3D beads and structures quite quickly by cutting a long strip of metal from a tomato paste tube, a foil lid or a piece of art foil. It can be as long and as wide as you wish. When creating standing vessels I tend to keep mine to a slightly shorter length than my needle.

Tightly wrap the metal strip around a pen, paintbrush or other small cylindrical object to create a rolled vessel or bead. You can also try rolling these by hand, but I find having a paintbrush to roll around helps with shaping and ensures I have a hole to easily pull a needle through. When you have created a handful of rolled vessels, stitch them vertically onto a base. The simplest way to stitch them is by sitting your rolled metal vessel upright on the base and pulling a needle through the centre. Put the needle into the base at the outer edge of the metal and then repeat on the other side so the vessel is sturdy and balanced.

If you have very wide vessels you can always add more detail in the centres, such as extra embellishments, sequins or even wire. Snipping the top of the rolled vessel can create a floral or coral effect. You may also want to experiment with changing the width and height of your vessels to create a textured, interesting surface.

Creased Metal Sequins

For another fun 3D technique, try creasing metal circles in different ways to create height and shape. I punch my circles using a large hole punch and then crease them into semicircles, folding each end into the middle of the semicircle to create almost a butterfly shape with two wings. These can be

A sample showing rolled metal vessel embellishment ideas created with rolled tubes of metal. I have varied the heights of the rolled vessels to reflect a coral idea. Some of the tops of the vessels have been snipped with scissors and embellished with wire shapes.

Creased metal sequin sample. Rather than just folding the sequin shapes to create a sharp 3D fold, I have used a paintbrush to roll the metal to make a softer 3D shape. The sequins here are created with tomato paste tubes and foil dessert lids.

couched, which avoids you punching the needle through the metal. If you do want to punch a hole and stitch any folded embellishments through the metal itself, use a larger needle and punch the hole before stitching. Metal can be slippery to push a needle through and you don't want to accidentally go through your finger instead! As well as folding metal and creating sharp, angular creases you can also think about softer folds that work well with thinner, more pliable metals such as tinfoil or art foil. This technique lends itself well to creating repeating motifs and patterns on fabric. The metal gives a luxurious feel.

Metal Zigzags

If you are working with recycled metal that has an interesting pattern, colour or even text on one side, it is great to create an embellishment that makes both sides of the metal visible. Try cutting a strip of metal. Again, this can be any width and length – a good starting width is something slightly narrower than your thumb. Take one end of the metal strip and twist it back and forth on an angle to create a zigzag pattern. You can play with creating large folds, smaller folds, even experimenting with whether the zigzags are pressed firmly to create a flatter embellishment or given more bounce by leaving some spacing to make a 3D effect. If you do this technique with a very long strip of metal, you will have the ability to create a curved shape rather than a straight line. This can be stitched onto bases by couching and going over the metal shape from side to side, meaning your sewing needle doesn't have to puncture the metal.

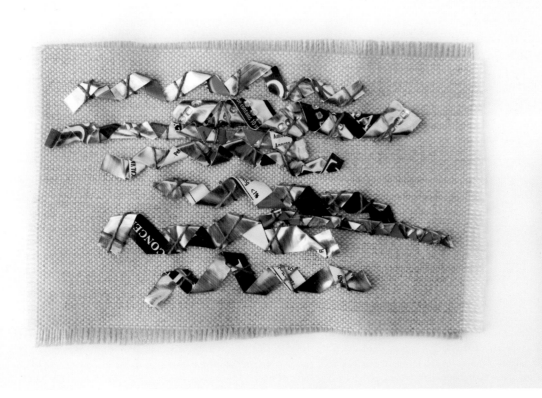

Example of a zigzag metal twist. This sample explores folding and twisting the strips of metal in different ways, varying the spacing, thickness and regularity of the twists. I like how you can glimpse the bright colours of the packaging with both sides of the metal strip visible.

How to Create Beaded Metal Washers

This technique will show you how to further embellish metal washers to give them a unique, colourful and decorative effect for then adding onto bases. There are numerous ways to change the results of the technique using different threads, colours and types of washer. If you would like to paint your metal washer first, you can do so by using spray paint, acrylic paint or even nail varnish to give a coating of colour on top of the metal. Alternatively, the metal gives a metallic shine and industrial edge to a project, which is a nice contrast with a soft thread.

MATERIALS NEEDED

- Various sizes of metal washers – I would recommend something with a fairly large inner hole to begin with.
- Small seed beads – for a bead with a larger hole, try cutting a paper straw into your own beads.
- Needle and thick thread, such as wool or embroidery thread with all six strands. (Make sure your bead will go through your thread of choice.)
- Fabric or paper base for stitching your beaded washers onto (something dense that will support the washer's weight).
- Scissors.
- Coloured wire – thin and flexible works best, such as jewellery wire (optional).

1. Tie your thick thread in a double knot around your washer, from the inside to the outside edge, so it is secure.

2. Thread your sewing needle onto the other end of the thread. Position so the knot on the washer is sitting at the top edge.

3. Thread your needle from the back to the front of the washer, coming through the centre hole of the washer to make a loop.

continued on the following page

4. Thread your needle through the loop and then gently pull the thread tight to create your first stitch. Push the stitch up to the knot.

5. Repeat Steps 3 and 4 again to create your second stitch. You may need to twist the thread so that the stitches lie along the top edge.

6. Take a seed bead or piece of paper straw and thread onto your needle, pulling it down next to the second stitch. You could add a cluster of beads for this step.

7. Repeat Steps 3 and 4 again. This stitch will secure your bead or straw into position along the top of the washer, creating a beaded edge.

8. Continue to repeat, creating two stitches then adding a bead or straw onto the stitch. I stitch around half of my washer – you can stitch more or less.

9. To finish, go through the last stitch with your needle twice, then tie in a double knot and snip off the tail thread.

10. For a simpler version of this technique using wire, simply wrap your wire tightly around your washer, threading beads onto the wire and adding loops and twists.

11. Repeat the steps to make different beaded washers, altering your thread colour, type of washer and patterns to create a collection of embellishments to use.

12. The beaded washers can be stitched vertically onto bases by supporting them between other 3D embellishments and stitching with a strong thread or stitching flat with detailed centres.

Finished beaded metal washer sample.

CHAPTER 6

RECYCLED PLASTIC

Plastic is one of those materials that you see everywhere, and it can be difficult to recycle. As much as you can try to avoid buying produce or anything that includes plastic, it is still a very tricky task to achieve. Instead, looking at alternative ways of upcycling and giving waste plastic a new lease of life is the perfect idea. I personally dislike throwing plastic in the bin and try to recycle it back into samples whenever possible.

There is a huge variety of plastic types available that react in very similar ways to fabrics and papers. Other plastics are more similar in properties to metals, which gives you lots of scope for using this material. The longevity of plastic, the bright colours and patterns that it comes in and its ability to be easily manipulated, all make it a great medium to use with stitch to create embellishments. It is an unexpected material that adds another element and a different tactile quality to stitched textiles. Unconventionality is the key here, and the more unusual something is, the more it is going to give an exciting result when tried with a more traditional technique such as hand stitch.

TYPES OF RECYCLED AND WASTE PLASTICS TO COLLECT

Plastic can be thought of as a clumsy, rigid or tacky material to use. It can be more challenging than fabric, paper and metal, but the rewards of upcycling plastic waste into something beautiful make it well worth the initial effort. The other benefit with recycling is that it is a lot more pocket friendly due to not buying brand-new and instead repurposing and making the most out of things you already own. When you think carefully about the varieties and types of everyday plastics that exist, there are multiple ideas, from thin, transparent, flexible sheets to crisp, moulded structures and everything in-between. This list goes through some of my favourites to begin collecting.

Food Packaging

Plastic food packaging comes in many colours and thicknesses. There are double-sided varieties and those with interesting logos, patterns and barcodes that can all be used. In terms of basic health and safety concerns, you must be careful not to use any food packaging that has contained raw meat and anything that has touched food or something perishable needs to be thoroughly washed and dried with a disinfectant to avoid contamination.

Outer food wrappers are a good choice. You may want to think about items such as crisp packets and biscuit and sweet wrappers – this sort of plastic wrapper is very thin, flexible and brightly coloured. Other ideas could include the plastic netting

Scrunched, layered and folded soft plastic sequins created from recycled food packaging.

from fruit, vegetables and wine bottles – the mesh of the netting is great for using as fabric bases as well as chopping into sequins. Also consider hard plastics, such as milk bottle lids, fizzy drinks bottles, cupboard basics like oil or vinegar bottles, and the plastic trays that often contain mushrooms, tomatoes or other small vegetables.

Transparent plastics are very interesting to work with; I collect cereal box liners, freezer bags, and pasta and rice bags. Double-sided plastics are a little thicker than your standard crisp packet-type varieties. Foods such as coffee grounds are often found in double-sided plastic, which is normally a solid colour on the outside and metallic silver inside.

Office and Home

Your office and around your home can be another source of easily accessible materials. Some plastics may look like fairly boring bits of rubbish, but there are many easy techniques to turn everything into something a little more special. Items such as document wallets, old bubble wrap, plastic notebook covers and plastic windows from envelopes are all great to collect. Some very thin plastics may deteriorate over time, particularly items such as plastic bags, however you can still experiment and play with mixing your plastic types to see which ones you prefer to work with.

As with food packaging, look for different textures, thicknesses and colours that you can collect. Some items may have been bought for another purpose and have scraps left over

Examples of various collected recycled plastics including shampoo bottles, mail bags, food packaging and coffee bags. There is such a huge array of colour within recycled plastics and you will find lots of patterns, text and metallics. These plastics have all been cut into easy-to-use sheets.

that cannot be used in the same way. When creating embellishments you often only need a small piece, so tiny scraps and leftovers are perfect.

Materials found in the bathroom such as shower mats, shampoo bottles, toothpaste tubes, rugs, anti-slip drawer lining and the inner supports from boxed goods can all be used. Any bathroom products need to be fully rinsed, sliced open and cleaned, and you may be nicely surprised by the plastic colours of some products. To make materials easier to store and to give more options for use, when collecting plastics that I think will be useful, I often cut them into sheets, strips or flat shapes that then can be stacked or rolled. Having a flat sheet of something is a lot easier than an item that already looks like a finished object.

DIY and Garden

I believe that you are upcycling if you use a product that was bought new for another purpose and you have some left over that will otherwise be thrown away. Searching for plastics in your shed, garage or greenhouse can unearth readymade embellishments that just need a lick of paint or colour to change them completely.

I collect tile spacers, plumbing washers, electric cable sleeve, plant labels, bag ties and cable ties, which can be found in different sizes and shapes. You can rinse and wash tile spacers after they have been used, and these are easily stitched by couching over them to attach. Nylon or plastic washers are often used in the plumbing industry; I have found packs of seconds that may have small flaws for plumbing but are perfectly usable for textile projects. Similar to metal washers but much lighter, they can be used in two- and three-dimensional ways.

Examples of collected industrial, garden and DIY plastics. You can see hard plastics such as tile spacers, bottle lids and tubing – these are very handy as they are ready to use as embellishments. I have altered the colour of some these plastics with synthetic disperse dyes or acrylic paints.

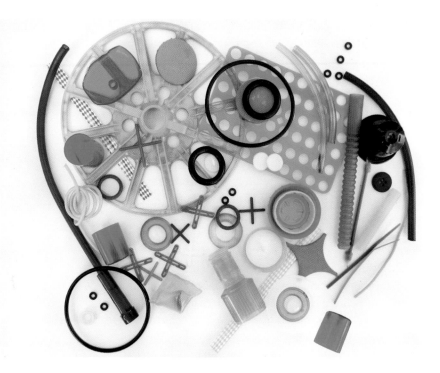

Scrapstores and Industrial Waste

If you have a scrapstore close by, they are a great place to rummage for unusual industrial plastics. If you don't, alternatives could include contacting local businesses to see if they have packaging, offcuts or anything similar that you could use or looking in secondhand shops, as mentioned in Chapter 1. Industrial waste could include large packs of plastic cones, washers and strips of plastic. Much of what you will find in scrapstores are offcuts, so shapes can be unusual and there can be flaws, marks or faults with products that may have to be cut around. There can also be excess product or waste, such as the negative of something else that has been cut out already.

You do have to approach the stores with a very open mind and really look at something's potential. I look for any plastics that are a good size for stitching. I check the colours and finish of the plastic and think about how easily it could be sliced or cut into other shapes. It is important to check if your plastic waste has a hole ready for stitching. If it doesn't, how easy is that material to pierce with a sewing needle? Weight is another consideration, although a lot of plastic waste is relatively light. Items such as buckles, buttons, cotton reels and cassette tapes are bulkier and heavier, but still work well as embellishments.

TRANSFORMING PLASTIC WITH INKS AND PAINTS

Plastics are available in a huge variety of colours and textures. This can be amplified further by adding your own marks and shapes to your material with inks and paints. Experimentation will need to be done with this technique, as when using recycled products sometimes results can differ. Lots of serendipity is to be expected!

I would always recommend testing the wear of a painted surface before committing to a large project or sample. One of the biggest risks with paint or ink on plastic is flaking. To combat this you need to look out for paints that also can stretch, such as acrylic paint, so that when the plastic bends, the paint bends too. Other paints and inks I would recommend trying include: spray paint, gouache, acrylic inks, nail varnish, chalk paint and household emulsion. You don't need to buy expensive paints so try out what you have around your home already. Very watery paints, such as watercolours or drawing inks, will pool on your plastic surfaces as they can't absorb and soak in like they would on paper or fabric, so these will create organic marks and textures. You can apply a top coat of PVA glue or even seal the painted surface inside another material after you have played with your marks and patterns. I tend to keep my painting loose and try not to overthink or to create a picture; instead I am aiming to add marks, textures and shapes.

Abstract-based patterns look really great when they are chopped or cut into more precise shapes, such as sequins and embellishments. There is no wrong way to do this, and you can paint away to create something that reflects your personality and ideas. Paints and inks can cause lot of mess, so before starting prepare your work surface with an old piece of fabric and a larger piece of plastic or newspaper, and have clean water and cloths on hand for any spillages. Also ensure you ventilate your space well when adding any paints or inks to a surface.

Various samples of coloured and painted recycled plastics. You can see a sample of lace fabric that has been painted through onto a plastic backing. Other examples have had paint randomly splashed and splattered onto their surfaces to create abstract, bold patterns.

- Paint and ink works especially well on transparent plastics, such as document wallets, cereal box liners and bubble wrap, and can give a lovely lace effect with opaque and transparent contrasts.
- Try keeping your brushstrokes loose and swirling paint or ink around on the plastic surface to create an abstract piece that can then be cut into different shaped sequins.
- Experiment with the types of paintbrushes you use. Anything can be a brush, from a fork to a snipped-off piece of cardboard box – everything is about making marks.
- Adding water drops to intense areas of colour will cause a resist effect with the colour pulling away from the plastic.
- If you are adding paint to other materials such as fabrics or metal washers, I often add a piece of recycled plastic underneath to catch paint drips. You will then get a stencil effect on the plastic to be used for another project.
- Don't overthink your patterns and marks. Go from one extreme to the other: try all-out maximalist, saturating your surface with layers of colour, or have a monochrome moment with some simple but solid, bold colour contrasts.

Die-cut plastic embellishments from a mix of recycled plastics painted in bright colours. When the abstract marks are cut into clean-edged shapes they create lovely patterns on the sequins.

CUTTING PLASTIC INTO EMBELLISHMENTS

The cutting of your sheets of material, whatever that may be – but especially for recycled plastics – is the moment that your rubbish is transformed into your embellishment idea. There are many ways to cut out your sequins from your plastic waste – some are more time-consuming than others and involve more equipment. I will suggest my top cutting ways and the shapes and embellishments that they are best suited to. These methods can also be used with other materials that have been mentioned in the previous chapters so far.

Freehand Scissor Shapes

Cutting your recycled plastic with scissors is the most simple and inexpensive way to create your sequins. You can choose the exact shape you want to cut out and create sequins like a jigsaw puzzle so that you have minimum wastage. As most plastics are fairly thin, you can layer up and cut through multiple layers at once to create a more time-friendly option. However, if you have a very large quantity of sequins to cut out, using scissors will take you a long time. I think scissor-cut shapes work very well for any embellishment I want that is more of an organic or natural shape, such as a petal, leaf or non-geometric form.

Shaped Craft Punches and Office Hole Punches

I have mentioned using these for other materials explored in this book so far as they are such a good beginner option, but they can also work successfully with some recycled plastics. The beauty of craft punches is that you can quickly cut out very sharp-edged and clean shapes, and avoid wastage by lining up your punch as close as possible to the last cut out. I do find punches to be temperamental and they can easily go blunt; stretchy plastics are like fabric and will just chew up and jam the punch, so they need to be avoided.

A scrap jar of plastic embellishments and small recycled beads and sequins cut from an item of clothing. The square sequins have been punched using a square-shaped craft punch to create a versatile shape.

My top tip for punches is to go for a very small shape, such as easily creating tiny circles using a regular office hole punch. The smaller the shape is, the less material in the cutting area, so you have more material options. Plastics such as vegetable containers, toothpaste tubes and flat plastic lids are good to try as they are nice and crisp. Punched sequins work very well for an inexpensive piece of equipment to cut multiple identical, clean-edged shapes for creating either a repeating motif or simple shapes to layer up.

Die-Cutter

A die-cutter is essentially a roller and platform with the sequin shapes themselves being determined by the die. If you are more committed to investing in equipment for large quantities of sequins, a die-cutter is a perfect option. Die-cutters are also great to use with fabric. I use a manual die-cutter and there are many brands to try.

In industry, dies are used for creating packaging and anything in quantity that needs cutting cleanly and exactly. The dies that will cut multiple materials are very thick and consist of metal blades sitting vertically on a base surrounded by foam or rubber. The blades are like cookie cutters in the shape of your sequins or embellishments. You lay your material on top of the die, sandwich it between two acrylic plates, and then push through the roller. The pressure of the roller squashes the foam, revealing the metal blades and slicing through your material.

You can cut most materials with a die-cutter and they are fantastic for being able to cut hundreds of sequins quickly and efficiently. Through personal experimentation, they are ideal for recycled plastics as they work with both thin stretchy plastics and thicker plastics that are hard to cut with scissors. Dies come in lots of shapes and patterns. I like the very simple shapes that give me the most flexibility for manipulating and making the sequins my own. The other benefit to die-cutting is the lovely negative pieces you get from where the shapes have been cut. These can be used for collages or background ideas or as stencils.

Die-cut offcuts – these are the negative shapes that I get left over from cutting out sheets of sequins. These are beautiful pieces as they are, and will be kept and used for small snippets of embellishments or as large sheets for layering and working into.

Alternatives

Laser-cutting services are an alternative cutting method and most services can be found online or through checking your local art colleges or universities. However, many services will require you to have a material data safety sheet for any new material to ensure the material doesn't release any harmful chemicals when cut with the laser, which can be tricky to obtain for recycled plastics. Laser cutting also requires you to be knowledgeable with digital software for creating your embellishments plan, but this does mean you can be very specific on your final embellishment ideas.

Using a paper guillotine can also work as a cutting idea for thicker plastics, if you are wanting angular shapes and sequins.

PLAYING WITH TRANSPARENCY FOR 2D EMBELLISHMENTS

I greatly enjoy experimenting with transparent plastics. They may seem boring, as they have no colour and in some instances they look completely invisible, but that gives them a unique look that you can't replicate with other materials. They have lots of potential for layering, building surfaces and trapping details. Good transparent plastics to look out for include: bubble wrap, document wallets, laminating pouches, kitchen bags, windows from envelopes and any clear food packaging from pasta, rice, fruit or vegetables. Transparent or clear plastics work best with 2D embellishment and sequin ideas. Cut out a selection of simple shapes using a method of your choice; I recommend cutting freehand or using a die-cutter for stretchy varieties and using a punch for crisp and hard varieties.

Layering clear plastics together so that areas overlap each other can build up dimension, but with a flatter appearance. Try stitching a layer of simple circles or square plastic embellishments onto a base with a small straight stitch, and then repeat with another layer, overlapping some sequins. You can repeat this as many times as you like – unlike with opaque plastics, with clear layers you can build and build and you will still see every single layer. You will find that really dense layered areas will become more opaque, creating new shapes and shadows. You can also try folding clear shapes before stitching to add further shapes and patterns.

Clear plastics can create lots of potential for suspending and trapping elements in-between transparent layers. To build up a beautiful surface with depth and detail, you can try sandwiching thread ends or offcuts between two sheets of clear plastic and stitching loosely around the edge to contain the threads. Keep adding layers, putting more elements to be trapped within each clear layer. If you are using plastic pockets, you can pop threads, scraps or other embellishments into the pockets and then stitch on top. These stitched pockets are lovely to use as bases, and other embellishments can be added onto their surfaces.

Clear plastic stitched samples. The left sample shows a stitched pocket of rainbow thread ends, to create a tactile plastic waste base material to stitch back onto and into. The right sample shows cut circles of clear plastic, layered and tucked together to create a repeat pattern.

How to Create 3D Stitched Plastic Lids

The simple milk bottle lid or washed-out plastic coffee pod can be transformed into a 3D embellishment to be used for samples. I think they look like mini corals, cities or even planets when completed, and they are really fun to experiment with. Some types of plastic lids can be more difficult than fabric to pierce with a sewing needle, so some patience is needed, but the end result is very much worth it. As with the metal washer technique, you can choose to paint your plastic lid beforehand. I tend to use them as they are, as piercing the lid to stitch it can cause flaking of the paint.

MATERIALS NEEDED

- Recycled plastic lid, such as a milk bottle top, coffee pod or bottle cap – it can be anything as long as you can pierce it with a needle.
- Sharp needle with a large eye, such as a tapestry needle.
- Regular needle with small eye and sharp point – I'd recommend a sharps or leather needle.
- Scissors.
- Long bugle beads, thin paper, recycled straws or plastic tubing with a hole through the centre such as cable sleeve, aquarium tubing or garden tubing. (You could also use the rolled metal vessel embellishments from Chapter 5.)
- Embroidery thread, any colour and type – thinner thread that is fairly strong, such as Perle cotton or doubled-machine cotton, will work best.
- Wool.
- Small seed beads and sequins (hole-punched sequins are a great size for this).
- Thread ends, wire or coloured elastic bands (optional).
- Base material: fairly heavy fabric, thick plastic or card.
- Embroidery hoop (if using a fabric base).
- Cork or sticky tack (optional).
- Glue (optional).

1. Using a clean and washed plastic lid, first make sure that you can pierce the lid easily with a sewing needle. Milk bottle lids are thin and easy to stitch, whereas other lids can be stiffer or more brittle, so you may want to experiment first.

2. Cut a selection of tubing or recycled straws to create your own beads. The trick is for the tubes to be shorter than your needle. I like to go with a nice mix of sizes, colours and types of media.

3. Knot a length of thread well to ensure it won't pull through the hole, then stitch through the base of the lid so the lid is sitting like a cup. This will also help to support all the vertical beads that will be stitched inside.

4. If you find the plastic tough to pierce, pre-pierce your holes for each tube using a larger sharp needle and push through the lid into a piece of cork or sticky tack. This will be easier on your fingertips!

continued on the following page

5. Thread a tube down onto your needle and pull it onto the thread so that it sits vertically inside the lid. Then pull your needle so the stitch goes down the outer edge of the tube, and pierce back into the lid to complete.

6. Repeat this by stitching through the lid on the opposite side of the tube with your needle, and then going back into the centre of the tube and through the lid. This will help to balance the tube and make it less wobbly.

7. Repeat Steps 5–6 again to add more tubes. You can cluster them together or spread them out in a pattern of your choice to create an interesting effect. You can add more stitches to create a pattern or to secure a tube if it is particularly tall or wobbly.

8. Another method is to stitch through the tube centre then add a sequin on top. This needs to be larger than the hole. Top with an even smaller bead and then go back through the tube centre, not through the smallest bead twice.

9. When you have filled your lid with vertical beads and tubes, you can go back to them and add another layer inside. Try pulling thread bundles, elastic bands or even wire down into the tubes to add fun and playful details.

10. To create a tassel take a length of wool, roughly three times the length of your tube, and make a bundle then fold in half. Come up in the centre of the tube and catch the bundle in the middle, pulling down the tube to make a tassel.

11. You can then stitch the 3D lid embellishment to another fabric sample, secured in an embroidery hoop, attaching it in place with a small straight stitch in-between your tubes. You could also use a dab of glue. The plastic is lightweight, so doesn't require a lot of stitches to secure it.

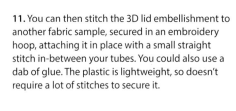

WORKING WITH HARD PLASTICS FOR 3D EMBELLISHMENTS

Hard or crisp plastics are those that are thick, tough and – if folded enough times – will snap or break. They can provide structure and are a great option for 3D details. Some plastic items made from hard plastic can be used without being cut or chopped into another shape, such as tile spacers, cable ties, labels or washers. Others in a sheet form can be cut into shapes of your choice using any of the cutting methods detailed at the beginning of this chapter.

Hard sheet plastics I like to use include washed vegetable trays, washed flat lids and notebook covers. Hard plastic can be tougher to stitch through as it is very thick, but it can be achieved with the help of a larger sharp sewing needle or using couching. This sort of plastic will react to the methods used to manipulate paper, but plastic has more rigidity and is therefore less fragile to work with. Experiment with folding or creasing hard plastic – this will create a white stress line on some plastics, which can add an interesting pattern.

You can create 3D petals for florals very effectively with hard plastics. Use scissors to freehand cut a large petal shape from a hard plastic sheet, pinch the shape in half vertically, then pinch back a small section on each side of the plastic in the opposite direction. When unfolded, this will create a structured petal with an unexpected texture. Poke a hole in the flat end and stitch around a central circle to create your own floral.

Creasing a flat piece of hard plastic will automatically turn it into a 3D shape. You can explore making tessellating patterns with any shape of plastic; creasing or folding and then stitching down with the flat end on a base. I enjoy exploring the possibilities of geometrics with hard plastics as I feel it fits well with the material structure. Simple shapes such as squares, and how these can be folded, interlocked and jigsawed together on a base.

I find that many hard plastics can be coloured with a dye suited for synthetics or nylon, such as disperse. As they are harder, they have a higher melting point than soft plastics so will not disintegrate in a hot dye bath. When trying to colour

Hard plastic sequins that have been created from a recycled notebook cover and soft cheese lid. You can see the difference in colour where the squares of plastic have been folded to make 3D shapes to couch onto the fabric base.

Hard plastic embellishments, beads and dyed plastic tile spacers that have been layered across the base to create a pattern. The beads are created by snipping small sections from a plastic tube.

or dye plastics safely use common sense and follow health and safety advice, making sure you have a well-ventilated space and the appropriate PPE, including a respirator and eye protection if using powered dye. There is a lot of serendipity in seeing what happens with different types of recycled plastic, which items will accept dye and which will resist it. Tile spacers, cable ties and plastic plumbing washers will all dye really nicely.

If any hard plastic is too thick or difficult to stitch through to attach to bases I often see if I can couch the embellishment, rather than stitching through it. This still creates a secure fastening if overstitched with lots of thread. This is a good technique to add tile spacers onto a fabric sample.

WORKING WITH SOFT PLASTICS FOR 3D EMBELLISHMENTS

Soft plastic is very stretchy and malleable and can react in similar ways to fabric when cut and manipulated into embellishments. It is fairly delicate and so needs to be handled lightly to avoid any ripping or splitting. There is a risk that this sort of plastic can deteriorate over time and become crumbly, so it is always worth experimenting and creating samples before committing to a larger project.

Scrunched soft plastic sequins, stitched with small straight stitches to create a dense area of texture. Soft plastic is very buildable and new layers can be pushed under and on top of existing embellishments.

Soft plastic can create soft, flowing shapes with an organic feel. It is very light so is perfect for layering. As this sort of plastic is often quite stretchy it needs to be cut by hand or with a die-cutter, as it will get stuck in any sort of punch. Soft plastics that I like to use include any sort of food wrappers, plastic bags, plastic wrap, cellophane and labels. Soft plastic is very easy to pierce and stitch with a sewing needle; using a smaller needle is always preferable as it creates a smaller hole so there is less chance of ripping the plastic. I also find that soft plastic comes in a huge array of colours so there is a lot of variation.

As soft plastic is very similar to fabric in the way that it folds and moves, you can experiment with creasing, looping or scrunching the plastic to create soft forms and shapes. It is very thin and is great for folding into small shapes that will unfurl after being stitched onto bases. For a great petal shape, curl a circle of fabric to create a trumpet shape and snip the end to create a fluttery edge. To create more depth with a soft plastic shape, you can fold and scrunch lots of shapes together and squash them into a smaller area. This will create layering and add dimension to a sample. Try stitching each shape with a single stitch, then pulling up layers and stitching another shape so that the plastic edges are pushed and moulded into textured forms.

As many food packaging items are made from soft plastic, you can cut out some lovely details with text or barcodes on, which are fun patterns to play with. The delicate nature of soft plastic means it doesn't want to have lots and lots of heavy stitches and thread though it, so often the less stitches, the better. One of my favourite materials to use for embellishments is recycled ground coffee packets. These are great as they are very soft, while being a lot less fragile than many thinner varieties. They are also double-sided with a metallic inner, meaning that you can play with both sides of the plastic when creating samples.

Stitched sample created from a recycled ground coffee bag. I have manipulated the double-sided nature of the bag by adding folds and tucks into my sequins, which reveal the inner and outer colours of the plastic.

CHAPTER 7

FOUND

Nature can provide beautiful and unexpected embellishment materials to use with stitch. I enjoy working with the contrast of weathered man-made materials and organic found objects from the coast, woodland or my garden. Rummaging for treasure when walking along the beach is one of my favourite things to do, as you never quite know what you are going to find. With natural materials, the elements such as the wind, sea or sun can provide a natural shaping or patina, or give an object a great texture. Unlike with the other materials looked at so far, found embellishments are almost ready to use and require less manipulation to prepare them for stitching onto bases.

Detail of stitched sample on mustard velvet, using scraps of lace, recycled plastic and drilled shell and metal fragments. The combination of materials adds contrast to the softness of the fabric base.

BY THE SEA

Beachcombing is a lovely way of collecting interesting materials to use as embellishments. Although you are not allowed to take away pebbles, stones or any material that is naturally a part of the beach landscape such as sand, other items that have washed up such as chunks of marbled sea glass, patterned pottery fragments or sand-bleached driftwood are all special treasures that are technically classed as litter. It is worth checking what the rules and regulations are in your area for picking items off the beach, just to be safe. You can collect some shells ethically from many beaches, always making sure that there is no living organism inside the shell and that you only ever take

a few. I tend to look for shells that are either small fragments that have broken off, damaged shells with holes in, or limpet shells.

Fishing rope and line is another material that can be used in interesting ways, and pieces of coloured plastic washed up from fishing boats. Picking up plastic is good for recycling and helping the beach to be cleaner, too.

Detail of sample creating a small composition piece using the natural shapes of found materials washed up on the beach, including plastic fragments, wire and metal elements.

An array of beach finds including pottery fragments, driftwood, shells, plastic and wire. You can see the huge range of textures and colours, with each individual material having a treasure-like quality. These finds can give sentiment to a sample if collected from a special place.

A collected rainbow of naturally tumbled sea glass, showcasing the array of colours – even multicolours – that you can get. This is one of my favourite materials to collect as every piece feels like a precious gemstone.

If you want a really good haul from the sea, the best time to go hunting is after a really high tide or more stormy weather, as the sea will have churned up lots of treasure from the bottom of the seabed. Always check tide timetables, and aim to go down just as the tide is turning from high tide so that you can walk along the tideline and start searching. Drier items such as driftwood can be found at the top of some beaches, out of reach of the sea. Always be careful when on the beach as tides turn quickly, so do your research and stay safe.

How to Turn Sea Treasure into an Embellishment

Many people will have collections of sea treasure, but stitching it onto bases can be more puzzling as, unless you are lucky, the pieces are all very solid with no holes for easy securing. You can use glue or couch sea-find fragments to secure them, but a more versatile method is to create a hole using a small battery-operated drill. This can be achieved fairly easily with some care, and will result in your very own pottery sequins or seashell beads. Driftwood and plastic waste are easiest to drill through and can be done with standard drill bits. Sea pottery and shells will require specialised drill bits, usually diamond-tipped, and are a little more fiddly to drill without cracking.

Sea glass is the most difficult material to drill and will require more specialised methods due to it heating up very fast, so I would recommend couching sea glass onto bases, not drilling. Always be careful when using battery drills, and make sure to follow the proper health and safety guidance provided by the tool supplier as well as wearing PPE for your own protection. Before starting this step-by-step guide, ensure you put on your eye protection, mouth protection and any other PPE as a basic safety requirement. *Never miss this step!*

Detail of drilled seashells stitched on painted paper. The holes in the shells have been used to play with stitches in different ways for multiple pattern ideas.

- PPE, including eye protection and face protection – safety googles and a respirator and mask are absolutely essential.
- Small piece of chunky wood, big enough to comfortably sit underneath your item as a base to drill into.
- Sticky tack.
- Items to drill: shells, sea pottery, plastic fragments or driftwood. A good guide for choosing a sea find to drill is something fairly flat and not too thick, if going through pottery or shells.
- Battery drill – this does not have to be expensive (I use a small handheld one).

- Fine drill bits – if drilling pottery or shells you will need specialised diamond-tipped drill bits to go through the harder surface easily and safely.
- Plastic cup or dish filled with approximately 2cm (¾in) of water.
- Marker pen or pencil.
- Masking tape (optional).
- Sandpaper (optional).
- Base, embroidery hoop and needle and thread – for attaching your drilled sea finds.

1. Put on your PPE, including eye and face protection – this protects against any dust, debris and accidents. Prepare your surface – this step should never be missed! You need to ensure your area is free of any clutter and the floor underneath is clear to avoid trips. Your drilling surface needs to be flat and sturdy – something like a table. You can also drill outside to help with ventilation.

2. Place a small piece of wood on your table to be your base. Place some sticky tack onto the wood and add your item to be drilled. Press down so it is secure – you do not want to hold it. Mark your item with a pencil to show where you want to drill. I would recommend drilling in the middle to minimise the risk of cracking.

3. Insert your drill bit into your drill, as per the manufacturer's instructions, ensuring it is correctly attached and ready to use. I would use a small bit. Position your battery drill on your marked point. It is easier to practise with something larger and work up to very small pieces of pottery, shells or plastic – smaller items are more fragile and can be fiddly to secure and attach.

4. Start drilling at a right angle, with the drill bit straight down into your item. Apply light pressure so the battery drill bit bites into the item. It can skitter on the surface, so keep hands well out of the way. If the surface is very slippery, such as on a piece of ceramic, add a piece of masking tape on top with a dot to drill through more easily.

5. Keep pausing to check the drill bit isn't getting hot. If it starts to feel warm, stop drilling and cool the tip of the drill bit *only* by dipping it into a cup with 2cm (¾in) of water for a few seconds. Never submerge the drill in water; only use a small amount to cool the drill bit end, and remove after a few seconds. Repeat if the bit is still hot, and don't begin drilling until it is cool.

6. If your item is getting dusty, pause the drilling, remove your item from the tack and place it in your cup of water to give it a rinse and remove the dust. This will help to clear your field for easier drilling. Then securely stick your item to the tack again and carry on drilling. Brush away any loose dust that gathers on the surface of your wood – you don't want to inhale dust, which is why face protection is essential.

7. Keep drilling until you feel the change in the drill bit as it gets to the other side. The vibration of the drill going through should feel a little more erratic as it comes to the thinner part – this is where you need to lessen the pressure, as you don't want your item to crack. Continue to check that your drill bit or item is not getting warm as you drill.

8. You will feel when your drill comes through the other side of the item into the wood. Pull the drill carefully up and out of your item, and rinse off any leftover dust. If the drill is stuck in the drilled hole, reverse the drill and gently pull out to avoid any damage to your item. This is the part when you can easily crack your item, so be very careful.

9. You may want to gently sand down your item with sandpaper, if needed – just be careful if sanding any patterned sea pottery, as this can rub off the pattern on top. Use a fine grit sandpaper or block and carefully sand over any rough edges around the front and back of the item, particularly around the drilled hole. Again, always wear face protection when sanding, to avoid inhaling dust.

continued on the following page

10. Repeat the process with any other sea finds you have. I find it useful to drill a few at a time so I then have a selection that are ready to stitch onto fabric. You can practise drilling different materials, as well as some softer items such as bits of plastic – these will be much easier to drill than pottery or shells. You can also change the drill bit to make larger or smaller holes.

11. You can stitch the drilled sea finds onto fabric, secured in an embroidery hoop, by adding either a stopper bead or sequin to the centre or stitching across the embellishment for added pattern. I like to layer up these sea pottery embellishments with other materials and fabrics to reflect the waves and sea. You could also think about stitching sea finds so that they are more three-dimensional and stand away from the fabric surface.

TIPS AND TRICKS FOR STITCHING AND USING YOUR SEA EMBELLISHMENTS

- Shells can be painted before stitching onto bases to create bright, colourful embellishments. I like to use limpet shells with eroded holes, which are bigger than a drilled hole and give me options for adding further details into the shell centres.
- Think about stitching shells so the inner is showing, rather than the outer. Mussel shells have a beautiful metallic coating inside them that adds shine to a sample.
- Use the natural shapes of the sea treasures to create your patterns. I like to create small compositions that celebrate each unique embellishment.
- When attaching a drilled sea find, you can pull your needle and thread through the hole then add a small piece of cut fabric and a bead, which is used as your stopper, before pushing your needle back through the same drilled hole to secure.
- Sea glass can be wrapped and secured with wire, which will contain it, and then stitched into place with thread, couching the wire casing onto your base. If you use thread on its own, it can slip off the sea glass.

Detail of drilled sea pottery embellishments.

A selection of samples created with found sea treasure on fabric and paper bases. The magic of using found materials is that you almost never get the same item twice, so every embellishment is unique.

WOODLAND AND GARDEN

If you don't live close to the coast, you can find some interesting materials to use as embellishments in woodland areas or even in your back garden. Materials such as fallen leaves, feathers, petals, and bark and seed pods can all make great embellishments to stitch onto bases.

As with collecting materials from the beach, be careful when collecting natural materials that you only collect or pick up what has fallen to the floor and not from a live plant. You can do as you wish in your own back garden, but parks, woodland and other areas may be protected by environmental laws, so always ask permission first. Also, always ensure that you can identify what you are collecting, as some leaves and flowers can be toxic and cause irritation or worse when touched – never pick any fungi. Organic material can be very delicate and so will need preserving in order to retain the colour and structure, otherwise it can grow brittle or mouldy over time.

Seasons can have a big impact on what you can find on your journey. Winter is great for sticks and twigs; spring for feathers and the beginnings of buds and greenery; summer for big, colourful blooms and foliage; and autumn for a rich carpet of rainbow leaves, seed pods and berries. Start collecting throughout the year to give yourself a catalogue of the months, which can give great inspiration for creating samples.

Examples of natural flora and fauna collected from my garden and whilst walking. Leaves and flowers are more delicate than sturdy sea finds, so I tend to collect in smaller batches to preserve items quickly and avoid any waste. Some of the larger leaves can be cut into smaller shapes and sequins before stitching onto bases.

IDEAS FOR PRESERVING AND USING NATURAL MATERIALS

There are many ways that you can preserve natural materials to use for textile projects and to create embellishments. The majority are very simple, and you may have to experiment with different ideas as they will all have different results. The key element to avoid with all organic material is moisture. Removing moisture is key to elongating the window of preservation and ensuring something natural will not decompose to sludge on your sample. Once your materials are dried and preserved, you can then cut them into sequins or use them as embellishments as they are.

Hole-punched leaf sequins and a stitched sample showing the effect as an embellishment. The leaves provide a soft, delicate feel to the sample with that essence echoed with the use of soft colours, small bugle beads and straight stitches scattered around the fabric. These sequins are very delicate even when preserved, but create a lovely autumnal effect.

Drying Natural Materials

- The first step with using your woodland materials should always be to dry them out. This should be done after your materials have been washed and then patted dry. Drying is what stops the decomposition process as it removes the moisture that causes mould.
- Less fleshy leaves, petals and foliage will preserve and dry out more successfully. To create your own flower press, You can press leaves and petals between paper towels with a stack of heavy books on top. Leave leaves for up to 24 hours and allow longer for flower petals.
- Leave seeds and seed pods out to dry in the sun. Papery cases can be pierced easily with a needle, but thicker, more three-dimensional seeds may need to be couched onto bases.

Preserving Leaves, Petals and Feathers

- Preserve dried-out leaves and petals by painting them with watered-down white glue, such as PVA. This also stiffens and strengthens them so you can stitch these materials onto bases.

- Another fun way to preserve is to trap a selection of dried leaves, petals or feathers in a laminating pouch and run them through a laminator. This creates a patterned sheet that you can stitch through as a base.
- You can achieve a similar look by sandwiching dried petals between clear sticky tape. This will allow you to cut around individual shapes.

Storing and Using Materials

- Some colours will fade over time – more so with exposure to light – so be sure to store dried materials out of the sun in airtight containers.
- If in doubt, test. If you want to use an organic material and are unsure of its longevity, appearance and fragility over time, carry out some small test samples.
- For a fun sequin idea, try using a craft punch on a leaf to create a sequin. This will be better on a fresh leaf. Dry the cut-out shapes before using.
- Twigs can be used as a long bead idea and couched onto bases. The large surface of the wood means you can add extra beads, embellishments or sequins when stitching to create a detailed sample idea.

Detail of stitched leaf sequins; you can see the delicate veins and textures in each leaf, enhanced with the thread colour and beading.

Striped fabric sample using couched sticks, seed pods and dried flowers, with added beads, fabric scraps and multicoloured thread for extra pattern. This idea of couching on found natural objects can be used to create woodland scene samples, and is great fun for playing with composition.

CHAPTER 8

DEVELOPMENT AND MATERIAL COMBINATION

Throughout this book, all of the techniques have been split into specific material chapters. Making and exploring mixed media in this way, as a singular material at a time, is really helpful for expanding your knowledge about particular materials and surfaces. You can focus wholeheartedly on one material type at a time and really try out ideas. Creating exciting samples is about learning to combine and start putting ideas and techniques together to create hybrid and developed work which is a reflection of you as an artist. Developing samples and ideas can be done in many ways, through trial and error, lots of experimentation, serendipity and mostly with practice. Combining mixed media, layering details and building surfaces with lots of elements brought together can start a whirlwind of creativity to lead you down another route for a new collection of ideas.

HOW TO START COMBINING MIXED MEDIA AND TECHNIQUES

When thinking about combining mixed media you can take simple starter approaches, looking at combining with contrasts, blending, tonals or highlighting. With contrasts you are looking at materials with opposing textures, colours or surface quality. Anything that has a strong contrast will really stand out and create an impactful, bold and zingy sample idea. I like to create loud work that is very full on with details, contrasts and colours. Contrasting samples are very 'shouty' ideas, where each material and technique is pushing out against the others to catch your attention.

With blending, you will want to think about combining materials or techniques that blend together or belong in the same family group, such as techniques with a soft, organic or strong industrial focus. Blended samples don't necessarily have to be subdued or minimalist but instead show a strong connection between the materials and techniques used, and echo that blended link throughout the sample. An example could be a floral sampler using papers, plastics and fabrics for creating petal shapes in various shades and tones – all of the materials used have that soft folded quality and hand-cut natural shaping.

Tonal combined samples have a focused feature of varied tones or shades of the same colour, which makes them very easy to build and make decisions about materials and allows you to focus on creating lots of detail and texture. You could, for example, create a blue piece of work that uses the same colours and shaped sequins – this tonal sample will focus on the difference in surface quality of each material and embellishment. This is a great idea for starting out if you are a little stuck, as it gives you a focus on collecting and putting those elements and embellishments together to build and develop an idea.

Detail of an organic composition sample with mixed media including a painted fabric base, ruffle couching, folded paper, plastic sequins and metal washer embellishments.

Contrasting sample ideas all are packed with embellishments, stitch details and bold colours that pop.

Highlighting as a combination idea is similar to contrasts but with more subtlety, using tiny flashes of another material, colour or texture to highlight specific areas of a sample. Like with tonal ideas, highlighting is a good beginner's step as it's all about pinpointing specific details and then adding them into a sample. You could think about a black and grey piece with a highlight of metallic silver threaded across in straight stitches, or tiny hole-punched neon yellow sequins. Balance is key, and whatever you want to use as your highlight technique or material should be a small taster injected into a sample.

Combining materials and techniques can be a tentative step between adding things you like and that have worked well together, and a bit of trial and error. Sometimes when you put embellishments together into a new piece, you may not like it at all. Having this outcome is not bad, or a failure, but a step in your development to create something that works well for you. Nothing is a failure if you pick up your needle and thread again and have another go.

Blended sample idea (right) and tonal sample (left). The blended sample uses soft, natural textured materials and colours to create a feminine, vintage feel. The tonal sample is visually striking, constructed in blue tones, with simple repeated shapes of embellishments tucked and bunched together.

Highlighting sample – the addition of the orange flecked embellishments is a contrast, but rather than being a really loud over-exaggerated pop, it is more of a sprinkle of concentrated detail.

Layering Embellishments and Building Details

One way that I work is rather than planning out what I am going to make and create in extreme detail, I adopt a layering process. Layering is another way of building surface and detail step by step but in a methodical, easy way that allows you to change details as you are working so that the finished sample is the most successful. Think about layering as starting with your largest 2D embellishments, then with each layer that you add, your shapes get smaller and the detail becomes more intricate. Three-dimensional embellishments can be added to give height and dimension.

As well as the size of your shapes, it is also important to note the opacity of your materials. A material such as a clear recycled plastic can be added later into the layering, as it will still allow the detail beneath to be visible. Mesh, laces and thin papers with variations of transparency can also be added in varied stages, creating peek-a-boo moments within a sample. Small details such as tiny embellishments, beads and decorative embroidery stitches will always sit on the very top as the last layer of a sample. They can be added over multiple layers to provide movement and direct your eyeline when you look at the completed idea. These are the intricate details that pull the combination of ideas, techniques and materials together and are a perfect final flourish.

COMPOSITION IDEAS

Every sample idea that you create will have its own composition. Composition is essentially how embellishments are placed on your base material in order to create a pattern, shape or image. When you are in the experimental stage, looking at singular materials, composition can go further down the priority list, with the focus being on getting something stitched onto a base, not really what it looks like as a finished idea. When you start to develop and combine ideas and techniques

further, you may want to think about how you then create patterns. This placement of embellishments and stitches can have such an impact on a finished sample.

Placement and planning can be something that prevents many people from getting started as they are worried about doing it wrong. Like with the other techniques and ideas in this book, composition can be broken down into very simple and flexible ideas; it does not have to be vastly complex or require prior planning.

Repeat

If an embellishment idea is working and you are happy with the outcome, repeat it to create a pattern. Copying the same motif or shape across the base material will create a repetitive pattern. You can look at keeping the spacing even to enhance the look of a repeat. To create a pattern that is less rigid, repeat

Repeat composition examples showing the variety of repetition that you can create. The top-left sample repeats whole motifs across the fabric base; the right-hand sample repeats a smaller element and scatters across the whole base; the bottom-left sample looks more organic, but still uses repeats to copy the looped thread detail across the sample. Repeat ideas can be simple, yet are effective placement ideas.

just a shape rather than a full embellishment or motif. You could also have a sample full of circles of different sizes and colours, layered in different ways.

Asymmetric

The negative space around an embellishment or stitch detail is key to the placement and composition of a sample. Asymmetric placement involves clustering embellishments in a pattern that concentrates on only one side of a base, so the overall design has a heavier and lighter side of detail. You can adjust the asymmetry by creeping small details or stitches out from the main cluster of embellishments. This fades out the placement and makes it appear to blend with the background and spacing around it. Asymmetric placement is a lovely idea for a focal sample that draws your eye to a particular area.

Central Detail

This is similar to an asymmetrical placement but with the main embellishments and stitch details clustered in the centre of the base, bursting outwards. This is a very simple idea to try – begin from the middle of the base and work outwards, ensuring your embellishments get smaller as you reach the edges of the base. The embellishments don't have to be symmetrical and can be different shapes, patterns and motifs, but the dense clustered spacing in the centre is what defines this placement. This is a nice idea to try when creating artworks to be framed as your eye gets drawn into the middle of the design first and then pulled outwards.

Asymmetric sample idea with the cluster of embellishments concentrated around the right-hand side of the base. Scaling down the embellishments and pulling details out to the edges helps to balance this composition.

Samples showing central detail composition ideas. The motifs and embellishments used here are very different, but each sample focuses your eye in the centre of the design first.

Organic

Organic placement has no rules, apart from looking organic and naturally occurring rather than planned out in a more regimented way. The best way to create an organic composition is to not overthink where the embellishments and stitches are going – try to let them grow and evolve. If you are trying to create an organic placement and it is starting to look more regimented, you can easily break this up by adding in another layer of detail or building on a pattern already created. This works well for samples and ideas inspired by natural forms, or when working with found materials.

Mirrored

Mirrored compositions involve the most precision as they have to reflect a pattern of embellishments onto the opposite side of the base to look both even and symmetrical. A top tip for getting an even symmetry with this placement idea is to create one side of your design or sample first, photograph it, then flip the photograph onto the reverse image and use that as a guide to put your mirrored patterns onto your base. Mirrored embellishment and stitch designs are used a lot in the textile industry, particularly onto application for fashion garments.

Mirrored composition idea – this placement is the only one that needs more planning. Using digital software can help you to get exact placement and create an effective mirror, as with this floral idea.

Organic composition, which is an easy one to build further with stitch and embellishments as the overall placement is very natural, not confined to specific patterns or motifs.

FINISHING SAMPLES AND IDEAS FOR DISPLAY AND USE

You can create sample ideas to trial techniques and materials in any size you wish. I tend to stick with smaller bases that are quicker to stitch together and create an idea. Once you have completed a sample you can finish it off in different ways, many of which will depend on if you have enjoyed creating your sample and if it is an idea that you want to develop further. Always make sure, when you think a sample idea is finished, that you securely tie all the loose threads on the back of your base to ensure all your stitched embellishments stay secure. Any knots that are looser can come undone over time, so try to tie them as close to the back of the base as possible. If you have used a base material such as a fabric with a frayed edge, you can leave the edge as it is, cut with pinking shears to prevent further fray, or attach a strip of clear tape to the fabric edges and then cut a straight line around the taped edge to secure.

You can, of course, keep your finished samples as loose samples to get out, hang up or use when you need them. I call my ever-growing collection my sample library, and it is a great record and source of inspiration to have to hand in my studio. If you want to try other ideas for samples that are really successful or have sparked a new journey of development, you can display them in various ways.

Using embroidery hoops as frames can be a fun way to create a round frame idea. You can paint or wrap your hoop and then secure by adding a straight stitch on the reverse of the fabric to draw in the loose edge. You can also add a card strip to the top of samples to make a hanger, which makes it easier to clip or bundle samples together. If you like the raw edges of your base material, you could create a wall hanging by wrapping the top of the sample around a thin piece of wood so the artwork can be hung on a wall. You could also create notebook covers with sturdier samples worked on paper or card bases, cut out shapes to make your own greetings card designs or even use small pieces as your own appliqué patches to jazz up an old item of clothing.

If you have a completed sample that you really dislike, don't be tempted to throw it away. Instead chop it up to turn it into sequins for another project, or work on top of the detail already completed to build your ideas. Use the sample as a learning tool to figure out why it didn't work and try again. Remember, every sample you make does not have to become a finished item; it can remain as a sample and will still have served its purpose.

Hoop framed sample with a floral twist. The wooden hoop has been painted black for a sharp contrast against the background fabric.

Collection of samples, placed together to create a sample gallery. When laid out like this, you can really see both the work in creating the samples and how many ideas are accumulated. Some samples can be developed into other projects; others could be selected to create finished ideas. These samples can be stored in a box or container, stacked on top of each other safely.

How to Create a Sample Sketchbook

A great way to display lots of individual samples, rather than having them as a loose pile, is to compile them into your very own sample sketchbook. This can be added to as you create new samples, and you could create different sketchbooks based on themes, colours or materials, which will provide you with inspiration if you get into a creative block. No glue is used for this idea, which means if you change your mind and want to take a sample out of the sketchbook, you can easily cut it free. This idea works best for flatter 2D samples that will not be damaged by being stacked on top of each other.

MATERIALS NEEDED

- Selection of stitched and embellished samples for your sketchbook.
- Needle and thread – a strong thread such as a Perle cotton or wool and a sharp long needle will work best.
- Scissors.
- Front and back sketchbook cover (optional) – this can be created from any material such as fabric, card or recycled plastic.
- Paper notes and extra offcuts and embellishments (optional).

 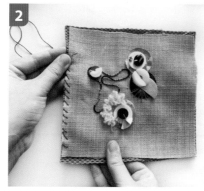 

1. Decide on the order of your samples. I like to keep my samples single-sided, which gives them some protection, rather than putting them face-to-face when the sketchbook is closed. If you have very two-dimensional samples, you could use double-sided pairs. Your pages do not all have to be the same size, but I put smaller pages at the front and larger ones at the back.

2. I work my sketchbook back-to-front. Take the very last page in the sketchbook and attach it to the next page on top. Trim any loose or wonky edges before stitching your pages together. Stitch along the left side only, with a simple straight stitch that goes around the edge of the pages, so the stitch is diagonally up the side of the sample page.

3. Take the next page and keep stitching along the left side in the same way with a straight stitch that goes around the edge of the page. Add each new page on top of the previous one. Stitching this way will protect the sample edges. You can keep your thread colour the same throughout or change it to match or contrast with your pages.

continued on the following page

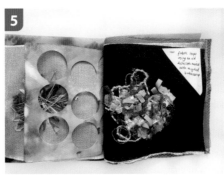

4. When you have stitched all the pages together, you can choose to add a front or back cover if you wish, or leave the first sample as the front cover. The stitching will make the pages flexible enough to turn, so you can see all of your samples together. Stitch any new samples onto the top of the first page to grow your sketchbook.

5. You can add extra details, such as stitching in labels to note down the techniques used for each page, as well as any extra embellishments. If creating labels, think of interesting papers, snippets from envelopes, plastic tags or other ideas to make them more tactile and fun. I like to include die-cut offcuts into my sketchbooks, as they add little frames or viewfinders to pinpoint page details.

6. For a simpler idea, stack your sketchbook sample pages in the order that you would like them to appear, then pull a needle and thread all the way through the top left corner of your pile of sample pages, from the back of the sketchbook to the front, and tie it in a knot. This will create a simplified sketchbook idea that keeps samples together in neat piles for easy organising.

How to Stretch and Mount a Sample in a Frame

If you create a sample that you are really pleased with and want to use as a piece of artwork, you can choose to lace and mount it in a simple glazed or unglazed frame. This works best for samples that have been created on a fabric base with spare fabric around the design, as you need the fabric to stretch smooth and wrap around the board.

The key with framing textiles is to try not to use glue if possible, so that you have the option for tightening or removing the artwork from the frame. The benefit of lacing samples to be framed is that the raw edges are pulled flat and tight, similar to how the sample looks if you stitch it in an embroidery hoop. However, you can frame without lacing if you want to showcase a sample with an undulating edge or an edge feature, such as a fray.

There are many different options for frames themselves. Box frames are great as they are chunky with a deep rebate, so any 3D stitched detail on your sample has space and is not squashed. You could choose to remove the glazing of a frame completely, which is a good idea for removing any barriers

Box-framed artwork from my 'Odds and Ends' series. This artwork is not laced as I wanted to show off the edges with the embellishments coming out of the central fabric detail, which is another display option.

or reflections that you get with glass. You can pick up frames very inexpensively at secondhand stores or order specific sizes and depths online. For mount board or backing card, I would always go for an acid-free option to ensure it is not going to damage your sample.

- Sample to be framed – this needs to have space around the embellished and stitched detail, so create it on a larger piece of base material.
- Embroidery hoop (optional).
- Foam board, 5mm (¼in) thick. If you don't have foam board, a piece of recycled brown corrugated card box will also work. I like to recycle foam board used for gallery shows to give it a second lease of life. The board itself does not have to be pristine as long as you can cut a clean edge.
- Scalpel or sharp scissors.
- Pencil.
- Ruler (optional).
- Cutting board or surface such as a scrap piece of board (always be careful with sharp scalpels to avoid injury).
- Sharp needle, pins and strong thread (such as 3–4 strand embroidery cotton or Perle cotton).
- Mount board or backing cardboard – this can be any colour; white or black are good for offsetting the sample and giving it breathing room in the frame.
- Frame of your choice to fit your sample.

1. Choose the size and shape of your laced sample. If you have stitched your sample in a hoop and want to keep its circular shape, draw around the inner hoop with a pencil on your foam board. Your board needs to be large enough so that all your stitching is on it, with the fabric edges wrapping around.

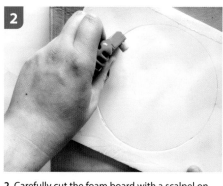

2. Carefully cut the foam board with a scalpel on your cutting surface. If you are going around a curved shape, try to keep your scalpel in a smooth curve, cutting away from you, to avoid jagged edges that can occur when cutting foam board. If cutting a straight line, it can be helpful to cut along a ruler edge – a metal one is best.

3. Lay your textile sample on top of your cut foam board shape and slightly stretch it out so it is smooth and flat, with all details laying nicely and no wrinkles or pulls in the fabric. Starting in the middle of the shape, push a pin into the edge of the foam board to hold the fabric tension.

4. Continue smoothing and pulling the sample to tension, adding pins around the edge of the board. You don't want to overstretch the fabric, but stretchy synthetics can be pulled more. Stretchy fabrics work best for lacing circular shapes, as you can really contour the fabric to the foam board shape.

continued on the following page

5. When your fabric is flat all the way around the foam board, flip it so you are looking at the back of the board. Smooth the fabric edges so that they hang over the back. There should be a small gap showing the board where the edges of the sample meet. Trim any overlap with scissors.

6. Now you are ready to lace your sample to the foam board. No matter what shape your foam board is, you will want to start in the middle of the board. Tie a large knot on your thread, which needs to be fairly long – I tie a double knot and leave a loop so it can't pull through my fabric when I lace.

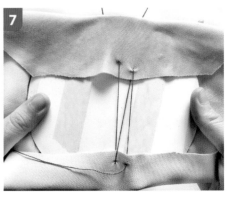

7. Push the needle and thread through the top edge of the sample and then down into the bottom edge, working from the middle to the outer right edge in a zigzag pattern, as if you are lacing a pair of shoes. Keep pulling the thread as you stitch to pull in the tension of the fabric.

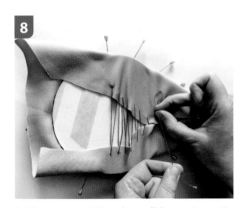

8. When you are at the edge, pull the tension again, flipping to the front to check there are no pulls or wrinkles in your fabric, then tie it off with a large knot. Repeat from the middle to the outer left edge of your sample. Don't worry if there are wrinkles on the reverse, as long as the front is flat and smooth.

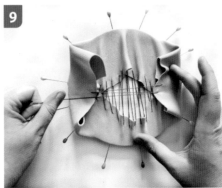

9. When the first horizontal lacing has been done, repeat Steps 7 and 8 again on the opposite edges of the fabric from the left to right edge. If you run out of thread, tie on a new piece so that it sits in the middle of the two edges and isn't affected by pulling the tension on the fabric.

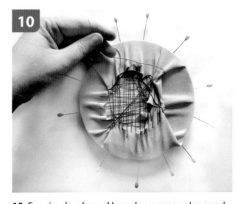

10. For circular shaped boards, you may also need to lace the diagonal edges of the fabric to ensure you have a nice smooth, round shape. For square or rectangle shapes, tuck the corners into the back of the lacing to smooth it flat. Again, don't worry if this looks a little messy on the back, as long as the front looks smooth.

11. Remove the pins to check that no fabric comes loose. If it does you can re-tension the back by adding in another lacing stitch. Check the front of the sample and ensure the fabric is flat, all detail is on the top of the board and the edges are pulled so the weave is not distorted.

12. Place your laced sample in the centre of a piece of mount board and stitch through the fabric, foam board and mount board with a straight stitch to attach in place. You can disguise the stitches on your sample by hiding them under a sequin edge, or even adding another embellishment on top so it looks like part of the design.

DEVELOPING AND MOVING FORWARD

Knowing when a sample is finished is a conundrum with no defined answer. It is something that you will learn to judge, the more you create. Mostly you will know when something is finished by taking a step back – sometimes leaving a sample completely – then looking again with fresh eyes. Ask yourself: does the sample look balanced? Are there any obvious unintentional gaps that need filling? Does any heavier detail need breaking up or lighter detail need building up?

Working with the process of layering is a good indicator for helping to judge when a sample is finished. If you always work from the biggest embellishments upwards to the smallest details, your mind will be prepared that the sample is nearly completed and finished. Adding on very small details, such as tiny embroidery stitches or embellishments, helps to pinpoint and break up heavy detail and adds a sense of balance to a sample idea. It's also okay to think a sample is finished, and then change your mind and decide to add another element to it – or even take it away if you have stitched on something that

13. Your sample is laced, mounted and ready to add inside your frame of choice. You can sign and title your finished work of art and hang it up in your home. If you have an unglazed frame, you will need to keep your completed artwork out of direct sunlight to avoid fading. You could even attach multiple laced pieces in one frame.

you feel is too much. I am a maximalist and my work reflects that, so sometimes I feel my samples and pieces actually don't have an end point. I could keep building and stitching them and they would grow and evolve with each layer.

Being creative, making and stitching samples and exploring new mixed media materials and embellishments is an exciting journey with many possibilities for development. You may be someone who finds their ideas grow organically, almost a trickle-down effect where one action of making will lead to a new idea and continue on and on. For those who are more of a planner, setting targets and choosing specific materials, ideas and compositions to explore may be the answer when moving forward and finding the next steps. What is key over anything else is that continuation of creativity – doing it because you enjoy it. The more you make, the more you will find your own unique voice as an artist.

The process is the joyful bit that shouldn't be overlooked or rushed, and is often the part that I enjoy the most. It is key to explore mixed media materials, which are more unconventional and unusual, as many of these materials don't have a set rule book for pairing with textiles, embellishments and stitch. Experimenting in particular can feel very luxurious. It is a green light to move forward, create and try out new ideas and samples without the expectations of those experiments working or there being anything at the end of it. That is completely okay, and it is a gratifying process to embrace fully and get stuck into. In my eyes, experimenting brings out your inner child and lets them just have fun!

Mixed samples that I may decide to work back into or leave as finished samples. It is okay if you don't know if something is finished. Samples are ideas in progress and so sometimes they may not need to be finished. The completed embellishments and ideas within the samples are those that I will take forward and put back into new work.

FURTHER INFORMATION

I have noted some of my favourite websites and suppliers to look for materials and tools below. For further information on my work and processes you can follow my socials online:

🔲 jessica_rosestitch

🔲 @jessicagradyembroideryartist

🔲 www.jessicagrady.co.uk

Scrapstores

Reuseful UK
www.reusefuluk.org

The Cone Exchange, Harrogate
www.coneexchange.org

SCRAP, Leeds
www.scrapstuff.co.uk

Percy Middlesborough
www.percymiddlesbrough.co.uk

ReSource CIC, Wales
www.resourcewales.com

Textile Foil Suppliers

Hand Printed
www.handprinted.co.uk

Embellishments and Pre-Cut Sequins

Josy Rose
www.josyrose.com

Recycled Paint

Seagulls
www.seagullsreuse.org.uk

Tools: Needles, Hoops, Scissors and Scalpels

Siesta Frames Ltd
www.siestaframes.com

Jackson's
www.jacksonsart.com

Die-Cutters

Sizzix
www.sizzix.co.uk

GLOSSARY

Appliqué: A patch of fabric or material that is added to a base. It can be applied to the front or back.

Base: The background material that embellishments and stitches are added onto. This can be paper, fabric, metal or plastic.

Composition: The way in which embellishments are placed and secured onto a base to create a design or idea.

Contrasts: Opposing colours, textures or patterns that stand out against each other, such as having black and white together on a sample.

Couching (Couched): Stitching over a material so that it sits on the base material surface and is not pulled through like a normal straight stitch.

Craft Punch: A shaped hole punch to cut larger sequins and embellishments from a range of materials.

Dead-stock: Waste or excess stock from industry, which is normally sent to landfill, such as fabric or threads.

Disperse Dye: Dye that will colour synthetic materials, including some plastics.

Embellishment: A decorative shape that is secured to a base to create a pattern, such as a sequin or bead.

Manipulate: Changing the way a material looks or behaves by using tools such as paint or by cutting, tearing, scrunching or folding the material to alter its appearance and shape.

Motif: A design created using a combination of shapes. It can be repeated across a base to create a pattern.

Perle Cotton: A type of embroidery 100 per cent cotton that comes in a range of colours and widths. It has a twisted look that pairs well with hand stitch.

Sample: A way to try out an idea on a smaller scale by creating a tester piece that documents a technique or material.

Sequin: A shape made from any material that is stitched onto a base and provides decoration and pattern.

Sharps: A hand sewing needle with a very sharp point which is great for using with tougher materials such as leather, plastic or metal.

Stitch: Another term for hand embroidery, using a needle and thread to attach embellishments to a base or add decorative patterns.

Textile Foils: Metallic foils that can be transferred to paper or fabric, using an adhesive substance such as double-sided tape or foil glue.

Mixed clear painted plastic waste sequins. These are all unique and a great layering option.

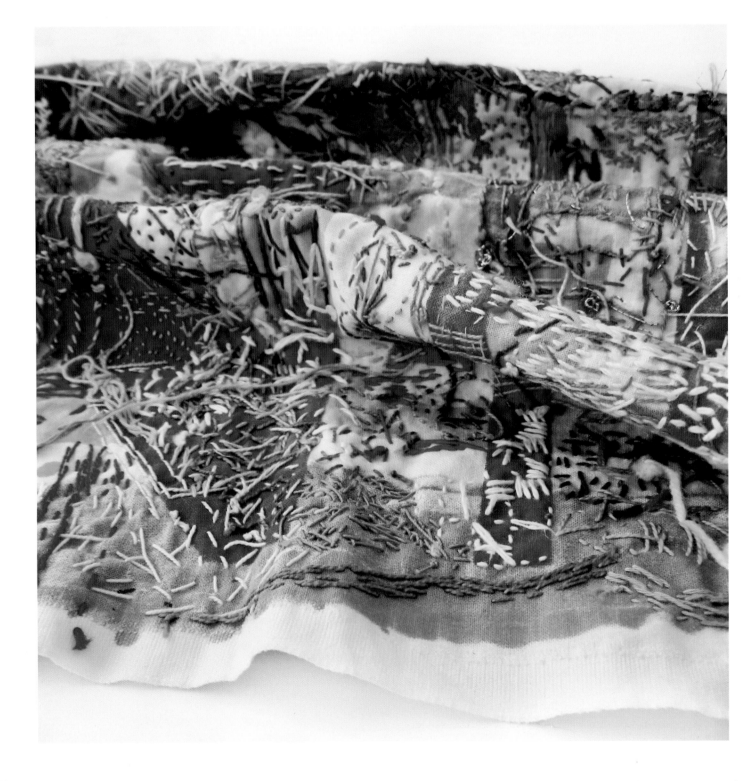

INDEX

Detail of the reverse of a stitched sample; the colours and threads stand out and create a second pattern.

First published in 2023 by
The Crowood Press Ltd
Ramsbury, Marlborough
Wiltshire SN8 2HR

enquiries@crowood.com
www.crowood.com

This impression 2024

British Library Cataloguing-in-Publication Data
A catalogue record for this book is available from the British
Library.

ISBN 978 0 7198 4223 8

Cover design: Sergey Tsvetkov

Graphic design and typesetting by
Peggy & Co. Design
Printed and bound in India by Parksons Graphics Pvt. Ltd.

ACKNOWLEDGEMENTS

Thank you to my wonderfully supportive Grady family who
have encouraged my career and love for textiles. My fiancé
Peter, who has always believed in me and has coped very well
with the explosion of stitch paraphernalia across our house for
the last year. You have kept me going with cats, cooked meals
and coffee! Thank you to the Crowood Press team for their
help, guidance and support along the way, to make my dream
of writing a book come true.